DEMOCRAT to DEPLORABLE

WHY NINE MILLION OBAMA VOTERS DITCHED THE DEMOCRATS AND EMBRACED DONALD TRUMP

JACK MURPHY

Front cover image by Kostis Pavlou.
Book design by Rachelle Smiley.
Editing by Stephanie Colestock and Rachelle Smiley.

Printed by Jack Murphy Live, in the United States of America.

ISBN: 9781981062522
First printing edition 2018.

www.jackmurphylive.com
@jackmurphylive
Email: jack@jackmurphylive.com

To Rachelle and my children,
I love you all.

Contents

Section One

The Journey

DEMOCRAT SINCE BIRTH

I WAS THE PRODUCT of an evolving nation. Both sides of my family were early 20th century immigrants to the United States. My mother's side was Irish, my father's was Russian. Settling in Chicago, they lived their version of West Side Story – a north side Jew mixing with a south side Catholic.

Being working class was about all they had in common. While my mom's father was stationed abroad during WWII, my dad's father returned home each night covered in axle grease. My maternal grandmother taught remedial English at a small local college. My aunts, uncles, and cousins delivered the mail, put out house fires, and arrested bad guys. They had calloused hands, dirty shirts, and everyone worked hard; this is who we were.

So when my parents came together, their immigrant heritages produced a novel result: me – an Irish Catholic Russian Jew named John Murphy Goldman. My dad always said it was the perfect politician's name, and maybe in the 1970s it was. Back then, it was bold for a Jewish man to marry an Irish woman, and I represented a new kind of American. We lit Hanukkah candles in the glow of Christmas tree lights, listened to Hebrew chants one day and Latin prayers the next, and there were bar mitzvahs alongside first communions. It was a little of this and a little of that, all mixed together to make something new.

My parents created this something new out of something old. In the '60s, Irish and Russians – even those who had been here for a generation or two – were still distinct from one another. They had rich, unique cultures with their own languages, customs, and histories.

However, these two nationalities were already united by the immigrant's story. Famine, war, and poverty forced them to make a decision unimaginable to most people. My ancestors on both sides boarded crowded boats with everything they owned, rode the cold waters of the Atlantic, and, once here, cleaned floors, hemmed clothes, and did whatever they could to scratch out a new life. Despite the risks, a scary new beginning in America offered hope and change over stagnation or even death. Eventually, my family's stories fused to make one which could only be found in the United States.

At age 13, I had my bar mitzvah, a Jewish ritual marking a boy's evolution into a man. Both sides of my family attended the Saturday morning service. As you might expect, the Irish Catholic contingent outnumbered my Jewish relatives by about 10:1. By the looks of the crowd, it could have been a Sunday Mass instead of Saturday services. The Rabbi, Barry Silberg, with his slicked-back hair and black robe, played to the crowd during his sermon. He talked of the 10 lost tribes of Israel, groups who were supposedly exiled after the Assyrian Conquest, and suggested that maybe, just maybe, the Irish were actually one of those lost tribes. Folks laughed at what seemed to be obvious pandering, but they welcomed the sentiment of unity. Whether it's true or not, Rabbi Silberg was able to make my two families feel as one that day. I stood on the altar as the product of two completely different histories, fused together in a way that felt like a true American story.

I

RECONCILING DISPARATE HISTORIES, the darkness back home, and the challenges of assimilation are common American threads. For me, bridging different worlds would become a recurring theme in my life. And as an adult I came to understand that the burden of reconciliation was not just mine, but the entire nation's.

Weaving different pasts together into new futures is an American archetype. Because so many of us came from different circumstances, a feature of the American experiment is the crisscrossing and mashing up of different identities to produce a new act in the play. Over time, we've had a tendency to meld ourselves into new characters whose stories ended happier, safer, and freer than they began.

But today it feels like the arc of reconciliation has bent away from unity, instead breaking hard towards enmity. Racial antagonism is on the rise. Women and men seem to understand each other less than ever. Globally-oriented ideas clash with notions of Nationalism, as born and raised Americans compete with new arrivals. The children of Isaac and Ishmael play out their ancient conflicts in modern times.

These people, ideas, and stories seem to be at an inflection point: either come together and move forward, or peer into a future where conflict reigns over resolution.

The national narratives are screaming. This is our make or break time. Will we swirl our traditions together to form the new core of American identity, or are we doomed to be "two lost souls swimming in a fish bowl, year after year"?[1]

In my youth, the nation sought to sooth the wounds caused by past generations of strife. The '60s, '70s, and '80s were a time when the country aggressively moved towards a more civil union – one where whites and blacks had the same legal rights, where men and women were offered the same opportunities, and where the laws and customs of our country evolved along with its people.

There was a national commitment to unity, but on the local level we each experienced this process differently. Progressive types were in the midst of it all, acting as civil rights activists, change agents, or leaders of a movement meant to heal historic wounds. The closed-minded fought progress, comfortable with the way things were and hopeful that nothing would change. As a child during this time, I was part of the solution. My role was to make new connections across color, class, and culture for the country's common good.

The march to civil rights and reconciliation led us to some extraordinary destinations. We're all the same now before the law. There's no more three-fifths of anything, no system-wide plan to render people ignorant and uneducated, no formal barriers keeping the needy from the basic necessities of life. The language of power and oppression guided us out of legalized discrimination and the politics of hate. Equality of opportunity has been enshrined in both law and practice. When Barack Obama shattered the black ceiling and became our first African American president, it felt like the final scene in an inspiring movie: America voted a black man to lead the country, and we were proud to do so. I know I was.

But sometime during the Obama administration, the energy around race bent towards darkness and decades of progress seemed to evaporate. Racial and gender animus began to worsen around 2011. Instead of coming together, we were now being torn apart. Obama's election was the end of a journey which began generations ago. Each passing decade built a stairway which helped lift him, and us, to the highest office in the land. But once we got there, it was as if we didn't know where to go next. Instead of stepping safely onto the landing, we stumbled and fell on our face. Peak unity was already behind us.

The 2016 election marked the end of the civil rights era. An arc which began even before slavery was abolished, it crescendoed through the 20th century, finally hit top altitude, and then came crashing down, punctuated by the inauguration of Donald Trump. The righteous work which aimed to free the slaves, restore their individual liberty, and enshrine equal opportunity under the law didn't deliver a harmonious new age where Dr. Martin Luther King's vision of a colorless society reigned. Instead, generations of effort delivered us burning cities, torch bearing mobs, and open street violence. The more we worked towards unity, the more it seemed to tear us apart. Though the language of race relations had tempered over time and racial resentment among all groups had diminished, its sudden resurgence took the country by surprise. While some people like to blame Donald Trump for this phenomenon, it's misplaced condemnation. He didn't create this moment as much as the moment created him.

Our nation's success was fleeting. For a country that may have thought it reached a new plateau of unity, this resurgence of conflict has been a jolt. The same forces which ended discrimination and delivered freedoms now work in reverse. A new religion of outcome equality devours liberty and redistributes oppression. The power dynamics haven't disappeared; they've simply been recast with new actors and scripts. Instead of fighting for freedom for all, it now seems like we're all just fighting for power – which really shouldn't be all that surprising, seeing as the power hierarchy is the indestructible backbone of life. The only change now is the matter of who is powerful and who is powerless.

And so here we are. In a time where the struggle for power is obscured by the language of equality, the American story of dueling identities clangs against the evolved reality of dominance. Reconciliation has been replaced by liberation, harmony moved aside for revolution, and reconstruction abandoned for dismantling. Talks of building things together have been muted by chants to tear it all down, and the chants grew louder than ever during the 2016 election.

2016 brought new challenges, new ideas, and created a new type of voter. Identifying as neither Republican nor Democrat, the nine million Obama voters who embraced Donald Trump feel the fault line of American culture pass through our middles. We are the last bridge keeping these worlds from cleaving apart and spiraling away into two unconnected universes complete with different languages, customs, expectations, and world views. We're not Republicans, so we're strangers in a new land, and we're not Democrats, we were banished just as we walked out of camp. We "Democrat to Deplorable" voters are a new breed, and perhaps the future of American culture. We've gone through the wilderness of exile to find our new home. In many ways we are the lost tribe of American politics.

Today, the country needs its own Rabbi Silberg, someone that can help find our commonality in a sea of differences. As tribalization takes over our national dialogues, we need to find that shared story which leads us back together. This book is meant to give a voice to the misunderstood Obama/Trump voter, to explain how one can make the perplexing switch from Obama Democrat to Trump Republican, and to give shelter to those evolving from Democrat to Deplorable.

The American story in the early 21st century has moved into the insurmountable crisis of the second act, with Democrat to Deplorable voters as key characters. We've seen both sides. We've lived among both groups. We've broken bread with true believers from both the right and the left, and we see just how far apart the worlds have become. While my life story, and that of America, may have been an inexorable journey towards unity, today's detour leaves us panicked. How we handle the next decade could restore our joint sense of mission or extinguish any last hope of an American togetherness.

In the process, our national narrative will resolve itself as either an epic hero's journey, or a historic tragedy.

DESEGREGATION

OOKIE CUTTER AND sterile, my childhood neighborhood was fresh-cut from the heart of a cornfield. An abandoned farmhouse stood defiantly at the center of the novel development, decaying amidst the new homes rising around it. Gone were the crops of the old way, products of a lifestyle passing into history. In their place emerged a new way of life.

Unincorporated Allen County, Indiana passed from farmland to planned development, and as quickly as the houses were built the newcomers came to fill them. We moved from Chicago in 1978 for the new pools, new parks, and new houses. It was a new era. My family bought the dream.

Like many other parents, my folks wanted me to attend the best schools possible. Instead of enrolling me in the neighborhood elementary school with my friends, they sent me to a magnet school deep in the nearby city of Fort Wayne. My parents were enticed by the advanced classes, liberal arts education, and foreign language immersion. At the same time, they decided to participate in a radical social experiment: racial desegregation.

Fort Wayne's elementary schools were racially segregated. Whites and African Americans did not attend the same schools. The Office of Civil Rights deemed the school district "severely imbalanced" and pressured the city to desegregate.[2] The first plan was to have compulsory bussing, where the law would require parents to send their youngest children to far away schools with kids they didn't know. Parents revolted, as neither African American nor white families wanted to be told what to do with their kids... even if the goal was theoretically noble.

After the first plan failed, the district took a new approach. Instead of coercing, they incentivized parents to make the election on their own. It was a grand bargain of sorts: the district met its goal and parents could choose what was best for their kids.

Magnet schools were established in predominantly-black neighborhoods, intended to lure suburban students with the prospect of an advanced education. And now, urban families could elect to send their kids out to the cornfields, where it was believed they would get a better overall education. Studies show that minority students perform better at integrated schools than segregated ones. The hope of something better motivated everyone involved.

In exchange for a 45-minute bus ride each way, I got the best teachers. In return for leaving my neighbors behind each morning, I learned Algebra in fifth grade. In place of a classroom full of my local friends, I was taught a lesson in group cohesion.

I may have been just a child, but I was a subject in a societal experiment. No one really knew what would come out of bussing kids in from the suburbs. Desegregation was a science project conducted in real time with real children. Elementary school seems like an early age to confront kids with racism, socio-economic divides, and cultural differences – but then again, not everyone in Fort

Wayne had the option to be so sheltered. The social lessons I encountered were as bold as the curriculum.

Our parents shipped us from our cornfield development into the crumbling city as a prayer for the nation. I didn't know it then, but hopes for a united America rested on our little heads. In cities all over, children like me were used as change agents, meant to mend the painful racial divides slicing through the country. Today, this seems like a heavy burden for a small child, but back then, it was a burgeoning new way of life. The nation had wounds to heal and we were the hope for the future.

As a kid, I saw things I didn't quite understand then, but they resonate with me now. For example, every day during recess there was a group of young men playing basketball on a dilapidated court with broken asphalt and chains hanging from the rusty rim. A few of them wore shower caps while they played shirtless in the Indiana sun. They were intimidating to me because they were grown men occupying our space. But basically, I just thought it was cool that they could play basketball all day. I didn't realize until later that able-bodied men hanging out on a basketball court during the workday was a symptom of a much larger problem. Back in my subdivision, the men all departed in the morning and returned around dinner time. It didn't mean much to me back then, but the image has stuck with me ever since.

The students were meant to be desegregating the city, but we were still kept apart. There were two doors: the bus door and the walker's door. To be bussed was to be white, affluent, and an outsider. The walkers were black, poor, and anchored. Every day, the loudspeaker would call out for walkers to leave this way, and bussers to leave that way. After a day of supposed unity, we peeled away from each other, eager to get home. Sure, the administration set this up as a logistical decision, but the symbolism stayed with me. Separate doors leading to separate lives.

As interlopers in their home, we didn't stick around. When the day was done, we returned to our little league complexes and swim teams while the walkers remained, left behind, our lives segregated yet again. I'm not sure what we were meant to learn from this experiment, but that's what stood out to me. The stark differences in our life experiences, our hopes and dreams, pasts and futures punctuate my memories. I remember the conflict, both symbolic and actual, between our two Americas.

I remember looking out the bus window each day. I watched the fresh suburbs, with their seasonal flower beds and water features, give way to the cracked sidewalks and broken windows of the city. I remember the alienation I sensed in the outnumbered local classmates, overwhelmed by swarming suburban invaders. Even as a child it struck me, and as an adult the questions remain. How much of our identities are based on race or class? Can we remedy years of institutional racism with forced intermixing? Does spending time together help or hurt our chances for unity? Can we overcome geographic, socioeconomic, and cultural polarization? Does 2018 look like the promise of the 1980s? *What have we actually accomplished?*

I didn't know it then, but this was the beginning of my journey. The early introduction of concepts like race, class, and culture into my young mind stayed with me through-out childhood and into my adult life. They revealed to me the divides in our country and the ways we attempt to solve them. The Spanish language immersion of my youth opened my mind to the existence of a global community. And the playground fist fights between white kids from the 'burbs and black kids from the city seared into my mind the embedded conflict of a multi-racial America.

CHOCOLATE CITY DEMOCRAT

"God bless Chocolate City and its vanilla suburbs"

- George Clinton, Parliament.

N OW MANY YEARS later, I live in Washington, DC, once affectionately known as "Chocolate City." For decades, DC was predominantly black, with a black mayor, black institutions, and even a Black Broadway. It produced its own music (go-go), its own slang ("you a bama!"), and its own condiments (mambo sauce). But over time, the black majority gave way to more diversity as the city got gayer, whiter, and more international. When Obama was elected in 2008, he staffed his administration with swarms of young activists and do-gooders from across the country. The influx of young people from every corner of America was a gentrification of sorts. But instead of getting bussed in from the suburbs, the white folks just moved on in.

Despite losing its black majority around 2011, DC is still a Democrat stronghold, 90% or more of voters here are Democrats. The Mayoral campaign is fought in the primaries, as no Republican can compete in the general election.

In 2016, Donald Trump mustered only 11,000 votes in a city of 600,000. Progressive, black, gay, and smelling like marijuana, DC is as blue as it gets.

The nation's capital is bustling today, but its recent past is marked by years of neglect and crime. The rebirth began in the 1990s, which is when I first moved into DC myself. I escaped the suburbs of Northern Virginia at age 18, moved to the city at my first chance, and landed in a cheap, sleazy neighborhood. My first one-bedroom apartment cost $600 a month. There were hookers in parking lots and abandoned buildings. Drug dealers operated openly in the air of lawlessness that hung over the city. Those were wild times back then, which was exactly what I needed.

I didn't end up in a fringe neighborhood in a changing city by accident; I made it happen. It was a willful expression, another desegregation of sorts. Attending high school in Virginia exposed me to open racism, a boring suburban life, and a monochromatic lifestyle. The pristine lawns and football on Friday nights simply weren't for me. I needed something more exciting, more diverse, and more authentic. As I got older, moving into the District was all I could think about. The first chance I had, I was out of the yawning vanilla suburbs and into the screaming city.

After a few years of enjoying the DC single life, I got married and settled down. The first house I purchased was wedged between a middle-aged black couple and family of Jamaican immigrants. Our shared walls represented our overlapping community. Bachata blared from one house, dancehall from another. We all lived on the same street in harmony, sharing food and beers and laughs with our neighbors. When my Jamaican neighbor had to work and couldn't attend her son's parent-teacher conference, my wife went in her place and reported back. To say thank you, she brought us homemade jerk chicken and a Heineken. We looked out for each other.

My home stood out as a symbol of change. Two of us lived in the modern version of a city townhouse, complete with an open floor plan and updated kitchen. It was bright and new, filled with the latest stainless steel and granite. Light shone through all the windows. But on either side – and really down the entire block – homes were run down or over-occupied. Eight people shared the home next door. A sad-looking house with a gravel yard stood opposite my home, which was sprouting fresh flowers and a garden. Bars still covered the doors and windows of most of the houses, a visual scar reminding us of the city's troubled past.

Being white, professional, and educated, some may have considered me a gentrifier. I didn't see it that way and I don't think my neighbors even knew that term existed. I was simply intent on being the best neighbor I could be; I wanted to bridge divides rather than create them. Yes, the economic contrasts were stark between us and our neighbors, but my wife and I saw ourselves as part of something larger. Washington, DC was coming out of a dark period marked by drugs, crime, and racial division. It needed all the help it could get.

A lot of people would be uncomfortable living in my old neighborhood. People tend to prefer living with those who are most similar to themselves. Maybe my early experiences with school desegregation gave me a unique perspective, which made it easier to live in a racially- and economically-diverse community. Moving from the suburbs into the city was a natural transition, simply mirroring my childhood memories. Living on the edge, where one part of city merged into another, felt like home.

When the 2008 election rolled around, I saw it as another chance to bring our country together. I proudly voted for Barack Obama, waiting in line for two hours to participate in the historic moment. The line at the polling station wrapped around the block, and it was filled with smiling faces and excitement. In a deep blue city, where one additional vote for Obama had no bearing on the election, casting that symbolic vote still meant something to me. I wanted to be part of electing the first black president. I felt the hope. I wanted the change. After the disaster of the Iraq war, the financial crisis, the housing bust, and eight years of Bush in DC, we were all ready for something different.

By the standards of the day, I was the perfect Democrat. I believed in equal rights. I believed gay people and women should have the same opportunities as anyone else (and I still do). In fact, I believe *every* American citizen should have equal protection under the law. Equality makes perfect sense to me. It wasn't until later that I would discover "equality" didn't just mean having the same opportunities. For some Democrats, it had come to mean equal outcomes.

Slowly and subtly, party alignment began to fade. The lines had shifted, and while I felt like I was standing still, the center rocketed past me as the Democrats lurched hard to the left.

In the '80s and '90s old line conservative values dominated culture. Exclusionary politics were the sole domain of the established GOP regime. To be on the side of freedom and equality for all Americans, not just rich white people, was to be liberal. If you were a punk in those days, you fought against the Republicans and the establishment. If you wanted progress, if you wanted freedom, if you wanted liberty – well, you had to be against the red. Going blue was the choice of the enlightened thinker.

I was always a Democrat and I had zero interest in changing.

DIVORCED FROM NATURE

MY DIVORCE LANDED on top of me like a pile of boulders. I lost my kids, my home, and a huge chunk of my income, all in one fell swoop. I knew that from then on, my kids would wake up most days without me. I'd go home to an empty apartment. Sure, the years leading up to the split were miserable, but I never gave up hope. After weeks of marriage counseling, both my now-ex-wife and the therapist said they were quitting. It was over. When the time came for me to move out, it was the only option left.

Obviously, the event itself wasn't entirely unexpected, but what followed certainly was. Family court, family law, and the difficulties fathers face with custody cases shocked me. It was impactful to see how the system seemed to favor women over men, and the number of ways that some women and their lawyers alienated fathers from their children. It seemed cruel.

Losing time with my children was, and still is, the most painful consequence of my failed marriage. The process of separating our lives and divvying up the kids like they were spoils of war, rather than tiny human beings, revealed other dark truths about society. I learned that marriage was ephemeral in the eyes of spouses and the law.

To me, marriage was a lifetime commitment, something that I would do one time and for forever. Aside from the vows where we promised each other eternity, I thought the marriage contract bound us equally under the law. It wasn't until I was neck-deep in an acrimonious split that I learned exactly what "no fault" divorce meant.

Astoundingly, people can just walk away from their "lifelong" commitments and take the children with them. As women initiate 70% of all divorces, this amounts to the bride kissing the groom with her fingers crossed in many cases.[3] I was always told that marriage was good for me and my family. But essentially, it is a one-sided deal, a lie meant to transfer resources from me to my ex-wife for decades without an equal commitment on her part. No-fault divorce is a relatively new phenomenon and cultural education around it hasn't caught up with reality. I wonder how different people's (especially men's) decision-making would be if they were told the truth growing up: "Marriage is good for babies and women, but for men, it's a risky deal with enormous downsides. Choose your partner wisely."

One night, alone in my new apartment, I opened my laptop and began searching for guidance. I needed to learn how to recover from the worst experience of my life. I needed to find answers in the midst of so many questions, and see if I could find someone, *anyone*, who could relate to my experience. In a divorce, you don't just lose your family; you also lose friends, neighbors, and your sense of community. I explored the wilderness of internet support groups in search of information and empathy. In my quest, I discovered other men who had similar experiences and felt the same way I did, and it was great to know that I wasn't alone. Even still, it was a strange journey on which to embark. Today, searching for new connections online is common, but back in 2009, it felt weird.

These days, meeting people online through forums and social media channels is normal. In fact, this contributed 'bigly' to the Trump phenomenon. Back then, though, the online groups were still fringe. Twitter was just for cat pictures and your grandmother wasn't on Facebook yet. In the real world, dads trying to get the most time with their children felt like outliers, and since few people seemed to care, huddling together on forums and messages boards was our best option. I learned that my experience wasn't an isolated event. Men across the country were coming face-to-face with society's lies and omissions. Our travails represented something larger, something beyond random incidents of misfortune.

Getting divorced, dealing with child custody, and ultimately re-entering the dating market at age 33 was the first time I realized something was really wrong with our culture today.

In the 90s, people could still go to a bar and meet marriage prospects. You'd go out with some friends, have a drink, and start talking to the people next to you. No one paid attention to how it all happened; it just seemed to work itself out. That's how I met my wife, in fact. We met at age 24 over beers, got married at 26, and were divorced by 33. I spent the entire 2000s deep in that relationship. We had two young children and a business together, and I worked my ass off for ten years. By the time my head had cleared after the divorce, I looked around at the world and hardly recognized what I saw.

I was Rip Van Winkle awakening from a deep sleep, returning to town for a homecoming but instead entering a new world. All the norms, mores, and methods of meeting people had completely changed. I met my last date in 2000 at a bar. Now, in 2010, single people didn't speak on the street; in fact, it seemed odd if you approached someone and struck up a conversation. Instead they used online dating services like Match.com and OKCupid. Tinder came around a few years later, and the dating scene has never been the same.

It took me time, but I figured out how to navigate the new mating market. As I learned the game's new rules, I also saw the first hints of wider societal problems. I was just a guy trying to meet people, but I ended up discovering something much more significant. Almost everything I learned during those early single years turned out to be symptoms of a more fundamental problem. I had no idea that exploring male-female dynamics would lead me to political commentary, but I followed the trail and here we are.

What I learned changed my life and taught me that life itself had changed as well:

1) New tribes can be found online. When I began learning about the new dating scene – how to meet someone and what to do afterwards – I discovered an entire online community of like-minded people. This process taught me that there were online communities for all types of issues, and people were coalescing around ideas and conversations over the web rather than allowing circumstances to determine their associates. Twitter and Facebook were in their early days yet, but websites, blogs, forums, and even mailing lists were steadily gaining popularity. These avenues brought people together around specific information, experiences, or feelings in ways I had never seen. This evolving dynamic would be critical to the Deplorable voter in 2016, as we were forced to seek information in ways we hadn't before.

2) Sexual marketplace (SMP).[4] Yes, there is such thing as a sexual marketplace. I hadn't even considered it before, my parents never told me about it, and people still push back at the idea today. However, a cold hard fact of life is that we're all competing in a sexual market place every single day. Men and women sort themselves according to their relative merits and evolutionary desires. Discovering this idea launched my exploration of gender dynamics and I learned how today's culture works to either stymie or promote certain types of behaviors.

3) Sexual marketplace disruption. Right after I discovered the existence of the SMP, I learned something else: the SMP is currently broken. Few people are happy with the way relationships form, and many bemoan the entire state of affairs. Ideas of traditional courtship, long-term monogamy, and dreams of a happy nuclear family are increasingly rare. The culture wars of the 90s nuked the traditional family as the ideal, and the concept of "it takes a village" took its place. Marriage age is up, overall marriage rates are down, birth rates are down, and extended singlehood is the new norm.[5] As of 2011, 39% of adults thought marriage was obsolete and over half of them were single.[6] Say goodbye to simple dating, mating, and marriage, and replace it with a libertine lifestyle of Tinder hookups, disappointment, and Sunday brunches. It doesn't take a social scientist to figure out that this is bad for the country in the short-term, and potentially devastating in the long-term.

4) Feminization of men, masculinization of women. One of the key complaints from both sides of the sexual marketplace is that women have become more like men, and men more like women. Hand-in-hand with the diminishment of the traditional family structure comes the swapping of traditional gender roles. Men and women – in prime fertility years, at least – come together to mate (or least act like we will). And traditional gender identities are what facilitated this for millennia. When you alter those roles, you get different outcomes. Traditional masculinity is now considered "toxic" and femininity is seen as a tool of the "patriarchy." Women have eschewed traditional marriage and a home life for careers and travel, and men have retreated into gaming, porn, and extended adolescence.

5) Social promotion of women over men. Today, women learn more, earn more, have more wealth, and are in better health than men. Early education favors girls, and boys are in a state of crisis. Young professional women outearn their male counterparts (at the same jobs) in almost every city in America. Women earn more college degrees than men. Women control more wealth than men, and they live longer, healthier lives. Men are falling behind in every single category, yet the national discourse remains stuck on a misconstrued "wage gap." If trends continue, men will fall further behind, exacerbating the already-damaged mating market. Women prefer men with steady jobs and education, and the available pool of suitable men for women to marry continues to falter.[7]

6) What upsets the bedroom, upsets the country. And so I began my exploration of the cultural forces working against men and women in their quest for finding love. Why was this happening? Why were relationships turning on their head? Why are traditional family values and dynamics cast aside for hedonism and "it takes a village"? Who promoted the idea that women's best expression of themselves was to be just like men, rather than championing natural extensions of their biology? Surely, men are aggressive and risk-taking by virtue of their biology, and women nurturing care-takers by virtue of theirs? ...Or not? Just what is going on here?

It felt like we were being lied to at every turn. Fewer people are happy, yet the narrative continues to double down. Women wonder why there are "no good men left," but it's because no one explained to them that the higher they moved up the professional ladder (and the more educated they became), the fewer men they'd find attractive. Men are told that masculinity is toxic, but when they adopt a feminine approach, their nights remain sad and lonely. Why are we operating under a set of lies which make us miserable? How else do these lies manifest themselves in our culture and national conversations?

I was surprised to find that my look into sexual dynamics would take me from the Tinder hookup app all the way to the presidential election, but here we are. The same forces which disrupt the SMP also disrupt college campuses, distort national narratives, mutate public policy, and ultimately reject science in favor of ideology. They pit men against women and create false notions like rape culture, which harm everyone – including, and perhaps most especially, victims of actual rape.

I know this seems like a lot to draw from simply observing how men and women form relationships. Believe me, I was just as surprised as you are. Since 2010, I've learned about gender feminism and its cousin, intersectional feminism, seeing how these theories have turned into practices which get in the way of normal human interactions. The deeper I dug, the more I saw how our national conversations, culture, and politics were shaped by radical theories with no basis in scientific fact. It just so happened that I discovered them in the context of dating. Today, I see how all of this fits together in the big picture, but back then, I had a few more unexpected upheavals to endure before I could put the everything together into one coherent worldview.

EDUCATION POWER

I WANTED TO change lives.

Life in Washington, DC had exposed me to dramatic income disparities. The rich in DC are some of the wealthiest people in the country, with five of the top 10 richest counties in America found in DC's Metropolitan area.[8] What seems ostentatious to the rest of the country is normal here. Range Rovers swarm the streets the way Honda Civics do elsewhere. Private schools, exotic vacations, and endless consumption are par for the course. A middle-class family can feel quite poor by comparison.

The segregation of rich and poor is barely held by a few city blocks. Make a few turns and the scenery suddenly changes. Majestic, tree-lined streets are replaced with cramped apartments plopped right on the sidewalk. Things like landscaping are laughable luxuries on the poor side of city, where a lack of grocery stores and access to healthy foods are a daily struggle.

Washington, DC's erratic education system separates the hopeful from the hopeless. The city is bisected by a large national forest called Rock Creek Park, and it divides the city in more ways than one. On one side, the schools perform at the highest levels. They have the latest technology, new facilities, and well-supported students. On the other side, schools are overcrowded, underfunded, and poorly-staffed.[9] They act more like holding rooms and temporary child care centers, rather than institutions that could change a kid's life for the better.

I always had an interest in social justice, and the inequity of the education system in DC bothered me. I examined the politics and economics behind school outcomes as my young children grew up. I could see how my own kids benefited from being on the right side of the park, but I also saw how kids unfortunate enough to be born on the other side were perhaps doomed from the start. The city wasn't doing all that it could, and it was young children who ultimately paid the price.

When the financial crisis of 2009 forced me into a career change, I turned towards charter schools. I had spent the previous decade developing residential and commercial real estate, but now I wanted to help charter schools build their own buildings. I began consulting on small projects, first advising with real estate matters and lending a businessman's perspective to school leaders. Within a couple of months, the students charmed me and the challenge activated me. I was soon recruited to join a school's leadership team and I gladly accepted.

The chance to help kids and challenge myself at the same time made the choice easy. Many people have tried and failed to fix the DC school system. Famous efforts floundered, the Michelle Rhees of the world came and went, and many skeletons of accomplished people littered the path to school equity. But I wanted to win, and I wanted to win for the sake of the children. So off I went, head-first into social activism, seeking successful outcomes for all students in DC... not just the whitest, richest kids on the west side.

My ascent was swift: Chief Operating Officer, Chief Financial Officer, and then ultimately, Executive Director. Within two short years, I had evolved from outside consultant to school turn-around expert. I took schools with atrocious test scores and improved them. I solved million-dollar budget deficits. I reorganized, restructured, and rebuilt two separate charter schools from the ground up. The teams I built turned around some of the worst performing schools in the city and made them the best in their area. We gave new ideas, new life, and a new hope to children who were once offered chaos. The Mayor held a press conference to congratulate us and the regulators were pleased. We were making education great again and everyone knew it.

The charter school world gave me the most difficult, most entrenched problems to work with and I solved them. I worked every day to serve the poorest, least advantaged African American kids in the city. When I say poor, I mean that 100% of the families earned 1/4 of the area average. For DC, that meant less than $25,000 per year for a family of four. While that may not sound so terrible in other parts of the country, in DC this means poor health, a poor standard of living, and ultimately, bad endings.

My schools were home for most of our students. Their parents dropped them off at 7 AM and picked them up at 6 PM. We fed them all the food they'd eat that day, and it wasn't great. Plastic-covered plastic trays with plastic forks, three times a day. It was all they had and all they knew. One year, we tried to implement a healthier menu. The kids revolted upon their first encounter with real cheese. "This isn't cheese!" they complained. "It doesn't fold in half." Cheese which crumbled had to be fake. Real cheese was peeled from plastic and folded neatly into soft rectangles.

Lots of our kids were homeless. We gave them money to take the metro from wherever they may have slept that night, and they often arrived at school with dirty clothes and no shower. The school had washing machines for them on-site. For too many kids, this was their version of normal. School was their home and their haven. The schools were beacons of hope in a sea of distress, a safe place to get an education and find a path to the future.

Once again, I was bridging two worlds, moving from one reality to another and experiencing both sides of the coin in the same day. For me, I returned to a safe, vibrant neighborhood each night, while most of the students remained in poverty and crime, surrounded by concrete and smothered by brooding orange street lights.

Talking with parents and students taught me a lot. I tried to understand their realities so that we could give the kids a chance at a better future. I learned a great deal about life in poverty and what it was like to depend on social welfare. I also saw the difference that a committed parent can make in a child's life. When I discovered just how many of the students had no one looking out for them, it broke my heart. It reinforced to me how parental involvement in a child's education just may be *the* most salient factor in their success.[10] This experience gave me a unique professional and social education, which informed all the work we did.

Despite what you might expect, my outstanding work wasn't met with accolades and job security. I didn't end up a hero, or even earn a dignified exit. The world was changing and eventually I learned my real lesson. Instead of a happy ending, my work in education delivered me a brusque lesson in the racial divides of our time.

At the end, they called me a racist and a sexist.

I

EVEN THOUGH THE Mayor, regulators, staff, and parents lauded my schools, the Board of Directors I reported to falsely accused me, suspended me, stripped me of my dignity, and ultimately fired me — in large part for being a white male.

You see, education in Washington, DC, is a woman's world. More specifically, it's a black woman's world. And while I had managed to easily navigate the cultural differences, I was always an outsider. A tall, masculine, white male stood out among a staff of predominantly black women and a handful of gay black men. When I first started working with schools, I was handed a guidebook on how black people did business differently than white people. I learned that black people value personal relationships over business activities, preferring to get to know someone first before getting down to work. I learned that the white way of doing things was white supremacy.[11] A sense of urgency, objectivity, and an emphasis on written documentation were now apparently tools of oppression, not just professionalism. While some of this struck me as odd, it was my job to adjust.

I hired, promoted, paid, and endorsed every single person who worked in my buildings. I was the chief executive and made all hiring decisions. I built schools which succeeded both in advancing students and the interests of women and minorities. We were winning together and my clout was growing within the system.

Press conferences heralded our success. It's rare for a terrible school to be turned around in DC, so when we did it people noticed. My reputation as a school turn-around expert was pristine and well-known, as our relentless focus on the mission drove eye-popping results. Fixing the schools, educating the kids, and creating an institution which could serve the community for decades was our only goal. This type of obsessive clarity is an essential ingredient to achievement and charter schools were no different. In fact, a school leader's indomitable will to win is by far the most important factor in any school's success. Performance falters when a school or any other institution deviates from its primary mission and begins to focus on other issues.

The Board of Directors of any non-profit is crucial to the organization's well-being. A board full of dedicated volunteers who are aligned with the Executive Director is the best scenario. A board staffed by low-commitment people who stay out of the leader's way is second-best. The worst is an activist board that has no idea what it is doing, or is motivated by something other than the mission.

People join boards for various reasons. Some want to help, some want to pad their resume or make professional connections, and others have nothing better to do at home so they volunteer and start meddling. But the worst board members come with a personal goal which runs contrary to the overall mission. They slither inside an organization talking the talk, hiding their true motivations, but when they begin to take action, their duplicity becomes obvious. Nothing will kill a school, a nonprofit, or any other organization more quickly than a Board of Directors who puts their own agenda ahead of the organizational goals.

Over time, my Board of Directors had evolved. The people who had worked hard and made tough choices alongside me had moved on to other projects. After all, we had made tremendous strides and momentum was on our side. All the key indicators were green lights. It was a good time to move on. But unfortunately, they weren't replaced by professionals with the same standards. The new board members brought their own motivations. They didn't care about our track record of success, or that we were nine steps into a ten-step plan. No, they brought their secret agenda and waited patiently to carry it out.

This was my first real-world introduction to "social justice warriors" (SJWs). SJWs are people who see the world exclusively in terms of oppressor vs oppressed, and everything they do is meant to dismantle the patriarchy, end white supremacy, rid the world of toxic masculinity, and so on. In their mind, because a white male is a white male, he is by definition a part of the "problem." Despite whatever track record he may have, an SJW believes the white guy has got to go. In short, SJWs are obsessed with identity politics. I didn't notice when the SJWs began to infiltrate my school's board. I was too focused on our goals and trying to improve the school. I didn't pay attention to the mounting threat. This was my mistake.

Two of them in particular began to cause problems. One, the board Chair, began disrupting our work by stalling votes on key decisions, sending me down unproductive paths, and poisoning the relationships we had with key partners. She sabotaged our work from the inside. Rather than stay focused on the mission, she distracted us, even though it would be the children who would bear the burden of her mistakes. The other SJW, another woman, wanted my job. She was the worst combination. She was motivated by her perverted sense of social justice as well as personal greed. Neither woman seemed to consider what was best for the students.

Both women wanted me fired and to severe the relationship with our most important partner. I tried to show them the errors in their directives, insisting that our education partner was crucial to success. After all, I wasn't going to let these women push me into making bad decisions for kids. Despite the stress, despite the acrimonious board meetings, and despite all the distractions, I held my ground. I'd worked for years to save this school and I wasn't going to let greedy misguided SJWs ruin it. I knew a showdown was coming – there was no chance we could work together when my eyes were on the organization goals, and theirs were on their own interests.

It wasn't like my performance was in question, either. In fact, it was nearing time to pay out my bonus and, according to the rubric, I was due nearly 100% of the allotment. I had exceeded almost every one of the metrics the board established; I did my job and I did it well. My teachers and leadership were returning, enrollment was up, our cash reserves were growing, and, most importantly, test scores were marching upward. Out of all the schools in the city, we were reaching our "at-risk" students better than almost everyone. At-risk students are homeless, on welfare, or just living in poverty – these were the kids we needed to save the most, and we were doing it. But it wasn't enough for those on the board with ulterior motives, because that's not what they cared about most.

Instead of rewarding me, they concocted a story to smear me. The board coordinated with a senior staff member and encouraged her to file a complaint, alleging that I created a hostile work environment. A hostile work environment exists when unwelcome comments or actions – based on gender, race, age, or other protected classes – interferes with an employee's ability to conduct their work. Because the staff member who filed this complaint was a black woman, and I'm a white man, it doesn't take much to read between the lines: she was calling me a sexist, a racist, or perhaps even both.

According to this complaint, which I was never allowed to see, I harassed African Americans and women to the point that they were unable to do their job. Apparently, I preferred to oppress women and minorities, rather than improve the lives of the poor children in my city. The truth was that I had hired, promoted, paid, and supported a staff that was virtually 100% African American, and mostly women at that. Over the years, I had hired hundreds of people; of them, I can only remember a handful of white people. Let's be clear here: I don't think I deserve an award for this, but I certainly didn't deserve being called prejudiced either. Helping my employees grow as professionals gave me as much joy as seeing the children's educations improve.

But in the end, it was for naught. Forget about our outstanding performance, forget about my excellent staff retention rates, forget about the years of service. With one simple move, they tarnished my reputation and slandered me with the worst possible words:

"You're a racist. You're a sexist. And now you're fired."

I fought it as long as I could, but there wasn't much I could do. The board elected to get rid of me and the vote split across gender lines. Even though they promised a full investigation, none ever took place. They pushed their false narrative of me being a racist and conveniently failed to confirm their allegations with facts. The board's lack of follow-through wasn't surprising. An investigation would have cleared my name and all they really wanted was to slander me. The remaining men on the board saw through the lies and several members resigned in protest. They took away my income and kept me from the work I loved with one simple line. It was all about power, and the women on the board knew they held the nuclear bomb.

II

By 2016, SOCIAL justice warriors knew the best way to achieve total victory was to point a finger and shout, "Racist!" It is indefensible. The mere accusation is usually enough to bring down powerful people. Once the lie is made, the end is near – no matter how dearly I wanted to hang on, it was over.

Losing my school crushed me. I had poured my heart and soul into helping those kids. My lifetime of bridging race, culture, and socioeconomics didn't help. Even though I'd spent every waking moment conscious of race and class, even though I improved urban education where countless others could not, even though I was the perfect Democrat in every regard, it didn't matter. I was now a "racist" and unemployed, simply because I was a white man in today's America.

In a world where we're told to be color blind, the color of my skin was something I couldn't shake. I was dedicated to creating a world where race didn't matter, where people were judged by their actions and character rather than by their appearance. And I was caught off-guard when the ugliness of today's racial realities reared up and stole my job, leaving my reputation tattered and my future uncertain.

In those days, I thought I kind of had things figured out: Work hard to be an ally, strive to lift up those who need help, do the right thing, and good things will result. But it wasn't enough. Nothing was enough. It will never be enough. Even though I thought I was ahead of the curve in understanding racial and gender dynamics, a new wave crashed into my naiveté. It left me not just unemployed but unmoored, bobbing in a confusing sea of shifting perspectives and expectations. Rather than my white maleness offering me an advantage, as I was told it did, it now stood in my way of affecting real, positive, social change.

I'll admit, it hurt. All at once, I went from successful social justice activist, to unemployed racist. The board's accusations caused me to take a deeper look inside, but what I found didn't align with what they said. I wasn't a racist, I wasn't a sexist. No, I was a man working hard for kids and I got caught in a new kind of turbulence. There were ill winds blowing and they took me by surprise.

White supremacy. Oppression. Institutional racism. Implicit bias. The national dialogue became dominated by issues of race and power in ways I hadn't experienced before. I'm sure these ideas were prevalent during the 1960s, but to me, there was a startling shift in the national mood sometime in the early 2010s. All of sudden, activists were looking to point fingers at individuals instead of at the 'system.' Someone somewhere just *had* to be the problem.

But it wasn't me – I wasn't the problem. I'd been moving steadily forward toward the ideals that had been instilled in me since childhood. And despite my experience with the board, I didn't give up hope. I was still a Democrat on the "right" side of politics and culture.

In fact, it wasn't until the President of the United States himself gave me the final sign did I realize my time as a Democrat was winding down, and a new future awaited.

CLOCK BOY

A T MY CHARTER school, we prioritized student safety. We considered how to balance risk with individual liberty, while maintaining an assumption of innocence. Should we have metal detectors? How do we manage bag inspections? What rights do the kids have? Do we want our students to feel like criminals when they come to school? We needed our schools to be sanctuaries, as most of our kids lived in high-crime areas. The schools had to be safe, but we didn't want the kids to feel like inmates either. We wrote thoughtful policies with all this in mind. After careful consideration, we removed the walk-through metal detectors and settled on handhelds for spot inspections. This seemed reasonable.

If a student brought a weapon to school, we called the police. A knife or gun would be met with instant detention and an immediate handover to the authorities. It seems obvious to say, but this was common practice in Washington, DC. All of our students knew the rules and we rarely had any issues, despite the prevalence of violence in their neighborhoods. Name-calling and fistfights were the extent of our problems.

Beyond neighborhood turf wars, there were national security interests to contend with. The country was on high alert, united against domestic terror. National campaigns and policies guided our thinking when it came time to make local policy decisions. In July 2010, the Department of

Homeland Security established the "If You See Something, Say Something Policy."[12] In it they describe oddly parked cars, open windows, and unattended bags as things to report. DC's METRO system is decorated with signs urging people to report suspicious behavior, and safety in our schools was just as important. We adopted a similar approach. Our policies were comfortably in line with the national directives and rational thinking, and other schools across the nation did the same. Protecting our kids was serious business – if we saw something, we planned to say something. It was the right thing to do.

I had no idea then that a policy which seemed so reasonable would ignite a national controversy.

On September 24, 2015, a student named Ahmed Mohammed brought an unknown device to his high school in Irving, Texas. It was a metal box filled with a spaghetti mess of wires and electrical components. He showed a teacher his contraption, claiming he had built a clock from parts. He seemed proud of his project and wanted people to see it. Ahmed's engineering teacher asked him to put it away because "it looked like a bomb."[13] His English teacher said the same thing. But then it started beeping. And beeping. And it wouldn't stop.[14]

The English teacher confiscated it and referred Ahmed to school administrators who, in turn, called the police. After 90 minutes of questioning, he was taken into police custody. In Texas, it is illegal to bring a bomb or bomb-like device to school; a deliberate bomb hoax is a crime, and his suspicious, beeping, metal briefcase looked a lot like a hoax. The police thought further investigation was necessary. However, after additional questioning, Ahmed was released and never charged with an offense.

Outrage ensued. The story exploded through social media. Within a day, a million people had tweeted with the #IStandWithAhmed hashtag. Celebrities, activists, and corporations jumped to Ahmed's support. Hillary Clinton, Mark Zuckerburg, and other prominent figures weighed in on his behalf. Google invited him to their science fair. Twitter offered him an internship. It looked for a moment like Ahmed was going to become a big star because of his clock. However, not everyone took Ahmed's side. Bill Maher said the device looked "exactly like a fucking bomb." Richard Dawkins thought the entire episode was hoax.

Plenty of people were confused by both the metal box and Ahmed's intentions (enough to warrant an investigation, in my opinion). However, this should have been a minor incident that was limited to local news coverage, especially after the boy was released without charges. Couldn't the national media give the police a pass on this one, given the extreme concern over student safety? It's not like Ahmed was convicted and sentenced to jail; his afternoon was disrupted and he got suspended from school. Policies are never perfect, nor are the humans who enforce them. Shouldn't we prefer our mistakes to be on the side of caution rather than neglect?

The entire thing may have blown over, except that President Obama then decided to interject. He infamously tweeted, "Cool clock, Ahmed. Want to bring it to the White House? We should inspire more kids like you to like science. It's what makes America great."

I felt personally betrayed. Here I was trying to take care of children and follow national mandates for safety, yet I (and administrators in Texas just like me) now became the bad guy. The president took time from running the country to insinuate I was doing my job wrong – a job which I took very seriously.

With one tweet, Obama discarded rational thought, support of teachers and educators, and public safety for political points. In a nation brimming with racial anxiety, the president alienated 100,000s or even millions of educators, law enforcement, and public safety professionals. And for what?

Obama underscored his intent when he alluded to Trump's "Make America Great Again" slogan: Obama wanted to divide the country. He implied that those who agreed with him were on one side, and those opposed were bigoted Trump supporters. For some of us, this was the first time we realized which side we were on... and it was Obama who put us there. Because the incident was rife with religious and racial rhetoric, the tweet became a dividing line in America. On one side, you had public safety and education; on the other, you had the president discarding hard-working Americans as Islamophobes. If Ahmed had brought that same metal box with wires to one of my schools, we would have done exactly the same thing as the Texas administrators. Not just because the government wanted us to, but because it was the right thing to do. *See something, say something.* Now, Americans who followed public safety protocols were somehow bigots. Obama and the Democrats lashed out to make ordinary Americans feel like bad guys.

The government had wanted us to be afraid. Worries of domestic terrorism drove policy, big budgets, and big spending. The War on Terror continued locally and globally.

Fear was in the air. Be afraid of bombs on the metro. Be afraid of bombs on airplanes. Be afraid of mass murders lurking in the dark. Oh, but don't be afraid of the wrong people (brown and/or Muslim) because if you do, you become worse than the terrorists... you become a racist. You're no longer trying to protect our children; instead, you're a bigot for suspecting that a metal box full of wires could be something dangerous. The media and the president gave us an explicit message that day: identity politics were more important than public safety.

The American mind space in 2015 was already filled with anti-white messaging. A new ideology called intersectionality, the promotion of white guilt, and media campaigns called "Hey White People" pelted some Americans with constant reminders of why they should be ashamed. Whether it was tearing down monuments, posthumously slandering politicians from other eras, or the racial antagonism from Black Lives Matter, the message was clear: white people are bad. The constant barrage was enough to make some long-time Democrats lose faith. It was bad enough that Facebook, Google, and other companies lurched at the chance to earn social justice points by offering Ahmed scholarships, internships, and other opportunities that no suspended white kid with a Pop Tart gun ever got.[15] They also capitalized on our fears and stoked further division for public relations. And then, President Obama – the man I voted for, the man I proudly stood in line to elect – piled on with his infamous tweet. My support had been wavering, but that was *the moment* that Obama and the Democrats lost me for good.

I

I HAD STRUGGLED with my own sense of white guilt. My past experiences with desegregation introduced me to concepts like race and class at an early age. I saw disparities in education, safety, and standards of living. When the bus took me from my middle class suburban neighborhood to the inner city, the landscape changed progressively from warm and welcoming (if not a little boring) to gritty, neglected, and even scary. It was a journey to the "other side," and the differences were clear – I understood that America was divided from an early age.

When the school day was over, I wanted to come home. Did that make me a bad kid?

However, these childhood experiences didn't make me feel like a winner. They didn't give me energy and lift my spirits. Instead, they activated my sense of empathy. I felt bad for those kids who remained in the broken urban neighborhood of Fort Wayne, Indiana. I felt the sense of loss endured by the residents of Chocolate City, as their old lives came to an end and the newcomers took over. I was safe and moving forward, while they were frustrated and seemed to be stuck. The contrast motivated me to do something and not just ignore it. This was one reason I started working in urban education. I wanted to stay and help, not just ride the bus back to the suburbs or count my profits while others despaired.

My white guilt translated into social activism and a commitment to the poor black kids in DC. I don't know if this makes me selfish or diminishes my efforts, but it's clear that my experiences with race and poverty motivated me to take action. It made me feel like one of the good guys. I took what I saw and transformed that energy into something positive. I wasn't one of "them," or was I?

It wasn't until President Obama posted that tweet that I ever considered I could be one of the bad guys. Who knows what his real motivations were with the message, but for me, it gave me the sense that I could never repent for my original sin: being born white in America.

I wasn't the only one who felt this way, either. Other people I talked to said Obama had seemed misguided before, but the decision to politicize Ahmed felt "sinister." They couldn't understand why the president would deliberately alienate Americans who were concerned about public and student safety. The Sandy Hook tragedy happened barely three years before this fake bomb incident. Who could blame school administrators for being overly cautious?

If Obama hoped to win votes for Hillary Clinton in the 2016 election with this tweet, his actions had the opposite effect. In fact, for some, this moment spurred a reconsideration of their entire world view. A young man from Texas told me, "At first, I was pro-Ahmed, but then I saw how the president and media manipulated the situation and it sent me down the pro-Trump path. Now I'm a completely different person."

Obama's Clock Boy tweet changed my perspective, too. I was already worried about racial tensions and what felt like an escalating division in America. I knew that racial, gender, and immigration issues were already separating us into two Americas, but now I had to choose between public safety and being called a bigot? There was really no choice at all. The president had made it for me.

I was out of the Democrats and into the political wilderness. But this wilderness wasn't just a metaphor. Being shunned by the leaders of our country had real world results. To be on the other side of Obama's wall meant absorbing vitriol and hate. If you weren't blue during the 2016 election, you were a red-hatted pariah. Racist. Bigot. Sexist. Xenophobe. The jacket they gave me wasn't mine, but I was cold and had no choice.

WHAT WAS I
SEEKING?

FOLLOWING MY DEPARTURE from the Democratic party, I was isolated. Old friends on Facebook blocked and unfriended me because I posted articles which questioned the media's narratives. Some of my family members (all Democrats) stopped talking to me and then hassled the brave few who stayed in touch. Certain topics were banned from family gatherings. Everyone was skittish. Politics had always brought fierce discussions at Thanksgiving – ideas and gossip were passed around with the cranberry and mashed potatoes – but now it was too risky to even speak. The forced peace among family members was imperative, otherwise rage would erupt and ruin everything. I was now that crazy uncle you only saw begrudgingly over the holidays.

I became an outcast, even though I thought I was following the standard life plan, doing what I was supposed to do. I believed in love and marriage, and for that I discovered the family law system and no-fault divorce. I believed in striving for social justice, but learned that succeeding didn't earn you any credits in the end. I thought my resume and reputation would earn me the benefit of the doubt, but I was in for a shock. Even just asking questions about the Democrats or their policies was enough to earn me a scarlet letter.

My bonafides carried no weight.

As the 2016 election evolved, I had no candidate and no party. My colleagues, friends, and family felt foreign. I was alone and in the darkness. Isolation felt like exile.

However, my sense of ostracization didn't come about as an accident. Though the various events in my life which lead me there seemed personal and individualized, they were part of a larger ideological landscape. Shifting attitudes toward power, the powerful, and an emerging sense that "something must be done" have their roots in new philosophies and ideologies that are spreading through society. Expectedly, politicians have seized upon them.

Critical race theorists, for example, believe that oppressive powers work through laws and institutions to marginalize minorities. They think that the government, social attitudes, and norms are meant only to prop bad people up, and keep good people down. The only way to liberate minorities from the institutional oppression they face is to tear up the existing structures and start fresh. This is a radical theory which began in obscurity but is now taught at colleges and law schools across the country. Hillary Clinton's coalition and her campaign language suggested critical race theorists would find a greater voice in a possible Clinton administration. If their goal is to dismantle existing power structures, what does this look like in practice? By sorting people into oppressed and oppressors, it seems obvious that I, a masculine white male in America, am always going to be seen as one of the bad guys.

Now, I'm a pragmatist in many ways. When I hear theories, my first question is, "Okay, so what does that look like in reality?"

On one hand, you have an emergent ideology which frames everything in terms of power dynamics: their goal is to take power from the powerful and give it to the powerless. On the other hand, the demographics of the country are changing rapidly and minorities, or the oppressed, will soon have electoral control of the country through sheer numbers. When taken together, it seems reasonable to assume a great power struggle is coming and the outcome is uncertain. What starts today as "Why aren't there more women in STEM?" could easily evolve into a radical reshaping of society, once the formerly powerless have enough votes.

Hillary Clinton embraced the oppressed perspective of this equation. She sought to rally single women, minorities, immigrants, and the disaffected LGBTQ+ alliance against a patriarchy dominated by straight white men. For a time, I wondered if her words were just lip service to identity politics, but the vernacular and the images she used made it clear. She was a woman, you should vote for her because she was a woman, and the people she wanted 'with her' were basically, well, everyone *but* me. Even her Vice-Presidential candidate, Tim Kaine, reinforced the message. He was soft, pudgy, and spoke Spanish – not exactly a masculine male olive branch to the type of guys who make up the "white working class."

I didn't want to think in terms of gender wars, but she forced me. I didn't want to think of the world in racial terms, but her rhetoric left me no choice. She handcrafted the perfect message to alienate me and people like me. Her campaign slogan should have read "I'm* with Her" *p.s. not you, Jack.

As the election tumbled forward, I still didn't have the answers. The open questions made me uneasy... angry even. What does a world look like when the "oppressed" finally become powerful? Do they throw off the posture of grievance once taking power? Or will there be scores to settle and retribution to extract? Is it even possible for the powerful, no matter which group it may be, to govern in a way that isn't oppressive?

I was mad to be thinking this way. In a world that was sorting itself around oppressor and oppressed, I found myself on the bad guy's team. I'd never been on this side of the equation. I had always been what they called an "ally." But that wasn't enough anymore.

Love and marriage were turned inside out. Racial conflict roared back. Men were the enemy, yet women could be men, women, or both at any time. Reality was falling apart. It felt like my operating system was stale and I was getting incessant reminders to update. I ignored the notifications for as long as I could, constantly deferring the painful process and hitting that "try me tomorrow" button until I was left with no choice. My mental model of the world needed a wholesale makeover. Hillary Clinton, the Democrats, and the steady march of oppression politics forced me out of the past and into the future with no direction.

We Democrat to Deplorable voters mostly stumbled upon Donald Trump. We certainly didn't seek him out. Many of us endured personal crises that opened our minds to new ideas, but few of us dreamt of a Trump Presidency. We were just alone and out there and needed someone to lead the way. Sometimes the best you can do is the least-worst, and in time that least-worst option revealed himself by way of a golden mop of hair in a golden tower.

In early 2015, no one was sitting around clamoring for Trump to run. By November 2016, though, Donald J. Trump cut through the chaos and offered hope to those who felt hopeless. Ironically, Trump, with his Make America Great Again was selling exactly what Obama had sold just eight years prior: hope and change. Hope and change... we always seem to be ready for hope and change, don't we?

A new uncertainty rose over the nation. The course set during the civil rights era seemed to be off-target. Equal rights and opportunities for all didn't deliver deeper unity and greater social cohesion. The country was exploding from the inside out, split into entrenched factions farther from the middle than ever before. An unnamed anxiety crept in where exuberant American confidence had once resided. Our foundation shaken and cracked, our future muddled and murky, our once-exceptional present faded to reveal a whispered truth: our grand narratives no longer held us together in pursuit of an American dream. Without reverence for our past, the future begged the question: if the American story brought us here – and here is an angry, resentful place – has it all been for nothing?

GOLDEN TOWER

WHY ON EARTH did he use that escalator? Donald Trump, billionaire, famous TV star and global businessman, entered the political fight by riding a slow-moving escalator like some sort of cheap, D list spokesmodel. It was the kind of move a novice actress would make at a car show. Something about it seemed off; it failed to emit the power or gravitas one would ordinarily link to a presidential candidate. Where were the 50 US flags? Where was the multi-colored sea of people behind him, reflecting his universal appeal? Why did he grin and give a thumbs-up like a cheap salesman?

Some pundits said you had to look past the surface message and analyze the deeper symbolism, otherwise you'd miss the entire point. Trump had forced the press corps to come to his tower, wait for him in his lobby, and broadcast the inside of his trophy to the world. It was a power play. "Look at me in my opulence and wealth, and come bend the knee. Broadcast my success to the world, as I ride down this stupid escalator."

But to me, I'll admit, he looked like a buffoon. I didn't take him seriously at first. I remember his half-hearted attempt at running in 2012 and figured 2016 was just another publicity stunt. Even though I was inspired by his books as a young adult, I wasn't convinced that Trump was sincere in trying to win the election. I figured he would screw around in the primaries and then announce he was getting back to business. Flirting with a presidential run would gin up interest in his shows, books, buildings, and other products (like water, wine, and steak). His goal seemed to be winning more sales, not the Office of the President.

From the beginning, Trump dominated in the national media. He kicked off his campaign with the escalator power play, and followed it with the 2016 election shot heard around the world. That, of course, was the infamous Mexican rapists soundbite: "When Mexico sends its people, they're not sending their best. They're not sending you. They're not sending you. They're sending people that have lots of problems, and they're bringing those problems with us. They're bringing drugs. They're bringing crime. They're rapists. And some, I assume, are good people."

The first news cycle was all Trump's. He commanded every channel, every show, and every talking head, sucking the air away from the 17 other primary candidates and presaging what would happen the rest of the campaign. When Trump says or does something crazy, everyone talks about it – his base grows while the media thinks they've slayed him. Repeat.

At that point, Trump's support barely registered in the polls; the challenges seemed insurmountable. Surely Jeb Bush, Marco Rubio, or even Ted Cruz would destroy Trump in the primaries. His efforts appeared futile. Yet, he persisted, tearing asunder imagined political divisions and opening the door for people to change coalitions. The national narratives were deteriorating and our collective mood was souring.

Whether Trump adroitly knew of the growing cultural divides or just happened upon them, it didn't matter. It's possible Trump simply found the right vein accidentally, his uncontrollable personality conveniently matching with the national mood and fortuitously aligning himself to the growing, but as of yet unnamed, insurgency building within each party. Or maybe his strategy was simply schtick: a cold, calculated creation meant to exploit the zeitgeist rather than represent it, a cynical power play rather than a call to duty. Either is possible, but does it really matter? The cultural tides were turning and Trump hopped on the right wave while others were still paddling out.

Trump caught almost everyone by surprise; few seemed to understand his appeal. Most pundits, pollsters, and hot takes failed to see the underbelly of how and why Americans relate to each other. Writers would talk about economic issues, or populism, or racism as a way to describe the growing rift between two competing visions of America. But they were just using words they already knew to describe a new phenomenon. The media is limited by their own frame of reference and their own identity. Because so many of them are Democrats, they can only see Trump through an antagonistic lens. Trump as president is a direct indictment of the Democratic agenda, an agenda which echoes within and influences the liberal media. It's no surprise they couldn't see this coming.

Besides, the Democrats were distracted by their internal struggle for power. Bernie Sanders stoked economic issues with regular Americans and Hillary Clinton shamelessly claimed the image of next in line. Bernie, the man of the people (true or not), versus Hillary, who deserved the election just because, set up a parallel fight for the tone of the country. Who would win the Democratic nomination was a legitimate question to the voters, but as we saw, not necessarily for the Democratic National Committee. As things progressed, it was clear that Hillary had the unwavering support of the political establishment and Bernie was the upstart. The Democrats' civil war reflected the country's dilemma. Should we continue with the ruling elites, nominating another dynastic ruler beholden to every corporate and political backroom in the country, or was it time for something new? Was the country ready for a deep cleansing or would the Clinton monarchy persist?

After eight years of promised hope and change, the country seemed more exhausted than ever. Like many others, I voted for Obama expecting healthy growth, a unique and uplifting experience which would unite us and propel us towards a post-cold war, post 9-11, post-racial era. However, promises of ending the Bush Wars and uniting the country faded as Obama's presidency concluded. The cultural rumblings, which exploded during the 2016 campaign and subsequent inauguration, had been percolating in the consciousness of America during Obama's terms. Campus unrest, attacks on free speech, fictitious rape culture, and the demonization of cis gendered, white, heterosexual men began during Obama's presidency and accelerated into the election. Questions on immigration, globalization, and race crescendoed. Obama promised the American people hope in 2008, but by 2016 his legacy was despair.

This new culture war peaked up through the fog of a confused and evolving nation. Democrat to Deplorable voters had given Obama our vote and he failed us. His Presidency fractured the very coalition which brought him to power, opening the door to a realignment few people saw coming.

Many of us didn't realize what was happening at the time. We felt adrift and unmoored. I felt isolated and abandoned by the party I had supported my entire life. Where I was going and who would earn my vote was to be determined, but one thing was certain: Obama had lost me, the Democrats had lost me, and Hillary had lost me before she even got the nomination. Really, she repulsed me. I could barely stand to hear her speak, much less elect her to four years of power. And thus, my divorce from the Democrats was a mutual decision. They kicked me out just as I realized I wanted to leave. It was acrimonious, rather than amicable. A permanent split.

The journey into the underworld – unanchored to a larger political group, disaffected with the status quo, and isolated in obsessed Blue America – reflected similar human experiences of transformation. Great journeys into the unknown are born out of need and endured with faith. My own party exiled me and millions of other Democrat to Deplorable voters, casting us aside as a political expense. As social animals longing for order and group identity, these feelings of loneliness and isolation are stressful. The wilderness has no sunshine, there are no safe and cozy shelters to hide under as the storm passes. There is only one way... and that way is forward. We mustered the emotional will to proceed alone and into the unknown until someone could deliver the answer.

Few expected it to be Donald Trump who would cast his light upon the needy. But as the election progressed, nefarious parts of America continued to reveal themselves. Our Deplorable voters, battered, isolated, and weary, would eventually rally around the one candidate who could brave the chaos and return us to order.

Ironically, when Jeb Bush dubbed Trump the "chaos candidate," he had it all wrong. The political establishment, including Bush and Clinton, led the forces of disorder. Trump was the hero here to save us. The enemies are not immigrants or foreign powers; our adversaries come from within, bubbling up from academia and permeating the institutions of our country.

Most of us didn't set out thinking we needed Donald Trump. It was simple, though: Trump came as the least worst answer to the left's cultural warfare. We identified a problem, a problem with no answer, and Trump was the one who reflected back to us the best understanding of our situation. He was here to fight, and we needed a fighter. The rougher edges of Trump's personality and policies felt safer than the dark ideology of the left.

Not only were we forced from our party, we were ushered into the hands of Donald Trump. Plenty of bitterness dripped from that double-edged sword. It's not like Donald Trump represented any obvious or coherent ideals. Supporting him is a grueling and often distasteful experience. But to vote for Hillary or simply sit this one out was impossible. The armies of division marched on the Capitol and only one general promised to fight back. When he asked us to rally, we were ready. The culture war conscripted us more than we found inspiration in a flawed reality TV star and shady real estate mogul.

One appeal of Donald Trump was the voice he gave to American nationalism. While a critic sees xenophobic rhetoric, a saner person may see a call to rise above the Democrat's divisive identity politics. The call out to Americans as a whole offers more hope than the battle cries for further intra-family warfare. "If you are American, you are with us, and let's make that America great again." The left can't get around itself to hear the urges for peace and unity in that slogan, but for those of us who thought Obama could (would) move us into a post-racial world, MAGA held more opportunities for unity than identity politics did. Americans come in all shapes and sizes and we must focus on our Americanism to bring unity.

The most powerful effect of Trump's slogan and candidacy was to paint such a broad image that we could project our ideal outcomes into the words. You could see whatever future you wanted in the MAGA slogan. I'm as guilty as anyone of projecting my dreams into the vague mantra. I wanted Trump to be who *I* wanted him to be, what *I* needed him to be, and it smothered all of the things Trump revealed through his outbursts. We rationalized and made excuses because Trump captured our imaginations.

As the campaign and election marched onward, Trump challenged our ideas of what was acceptable and laid clear the cost of electing him. Yet, the risks of anyone else winning were too great. Trump losing was worse than Trump winning. Armed with a vague offer of hope and change, MAGA style, Trump was our guy and we stuck with him. What came after that remained to be seen.

ELECTION NIGHT

THE NEVER-ENDING PRESIDENTIAL campaigns were careening towards one alleged apocalypse or the other. A victory for Donald Trump was the historical equivalent of welcoming a new Hitler. A Hillary win would end American democracy with a corrupt monarchy headed by felon and a grifter. If the various campaigns were to be believed, the election we faced in 2016 was not a choice between the two best options, but rather a dilemma between toxic leftovers. As the race concluded, the polls predicted Hillary the obvious winner.

When my girlfriend and I sat down to watch the coverage on election night, I told her, "It's been a good run and a lot of fun, but there's no way he can really win." The election felt like a formality. I was resigned to a Hillary presidency, despite publicly supporting Trump. I had been telling friends and family throughout the campaign that Trump was going to win, but I always maintained some doubts. Hell, there were times I doubted if he even *wanted* to be president.

But I was wrong. My doubt crept in because I still had one ear to the mass media, allowing their lies and agenda to leak into my consciousness. Even as I had my guard up against their bias, the repetition and consistency wormed into my head and left a seed of doubt... one which was growing as election night kicked off.

To keep busy during the extended election night coverage, my girlfriend and I tried our hand at making fresh baguettes for the first time. Each step of the process brought us back into the kitchen, away from the TV, to create something with our hands. The smell of fresh yeast and flour filled our kitchen while the TV filled the living room with polls and predictions. We made the first batch of dough and let it rise.

In the year leading up to the election, I had begun to take Twitter more seriously. My account, @jackmurphylive, had about 1,000 followers in November 2016. I'd tweeted about relationships, politics, and things we did around the house, such as baking bread. Election night was a chance for me to live-tweet the end of the presidential campaign and show off my new-found baking skills. It was fun to mix in real life with the political drama – my followers and I were into it.

We needed a distraction that night, after all. The prospect of a Clinton administration was depressing. No matter how I looked at it, four (or eight) more years of progressive Democratic rule meant things were going to get worse, way worse. If it seemed tensions were high at the end of the Obama era, it was nothing compared to what I thought a Hillary presidency would do to America. Baking bread got us away from the television and into the kitchen. The next four years would probably be filled with same kind of necessary distractions.

Results started to come in and the usual suspects broke exactly how we had expected. The blue northeast delivered for Hillary and the south for Trump. The easiest calls came first, of course. Just like my baguettes, however, this night was going to come in stages. The dough rose in the kitchen and set the foundation, just as South Carolina, Kentucky, and Georgia set the base for Trump.

There was still nothing shocking when we returned to the living room. This was going to be a late night: the swing states were going to be close, and early calls were not going to come on Pennsylvania, Ohio, Wisconsin, North Carolina, or Florida. But they were in play, which was Hillary's worst nightmare.

Other writers have outlined her failures in those key states. Her impenetrable blue wall in the Midwest was vulnerable in a way that her campaign never anticipated. People say she failed those states by not visiting enough or spending enough money, but to me, I think the bread was baked (as it were) long before election night. The inexorable march of globalism, immigration, feminist overreach, and political correctness had already alienated the "normal" people behind Hillary's blue wall. The 21st century version of ground game – trolling by social media armies – broadcast the messages to those open to listening, and delivered enough outrage to flip the states from blue to red. Hillary couldn't have done much.

Focused handling of industrial Midwest couldn't erase feelings which had been building for years. Just like me and my first attempt at baking baguettes, the voters in the Midwest were up for something new. They wanted a new challenge which could deliver them something amazing and authentic. Or perhaps flat, dry, and burnt... only time would tell. My dough rose with the vote totals, bit by bit.

We cut the dough into three sections, rolled them into baguette shape, scored the top with a knife, sprayed them with water, and set them in the oven. This was the moment of truth. The next 20 minutes would reveal whether or not I was able to take raw unfinished ingredients and turn them into fresh bread right there in my home. As I closed the door to the oven, full of hope and change, the early results for Wisconsin were announced on CNN. Trump was winning. He had a chance.

The heads on TV breathlessly recapped each additional piece of news, but none of them seemed to put it all together. They were terrified. To them, they saw their reputations as political experts going down the tubes along with the country. With one pull of the lever, Trump sent the critics down the toilet along with their predictions and polls and prognostications. For them to report of Trump's victory in progress on election night must have felt like describing their own intellectual death in front of millions of people. Each new vote that fell to Trump was another strike against their reputation. Trump was killing the media and winning the country.

But back to my bread.

I couldn't have timed it any better. Just as I was pulling the bread from the oven the TV news channels were beginning to call things for Trump. Key states were falling. Wisconsin breaking for Trump was when I finally began to realize: *it was happening*. I had fresh-baked baguettes and a house which smelled like a bakery, to go along with a new president and new era in American life. Smearing a slice with warm butter and eating the first savory bite was almost as satisfying as hearing, "OHIO GOES FOR TRUMP!" coming from the living room.

The night turned and the nervousness evaporated. Despite telling everyone I knew that Trump was going to win because of his mastery of the current zeitgeist, I still had my doubts. Donald Trump?! Even after all the nonsense, the pussy grab incident, the Mexican rapists gambit, the alleged mocking of a disabled reporter... after all of that, Trump was going to win. My girlfriend and I ate up all that bread as our energy levels rose. It was now well after midnight and we wanted to celebrate. There was only one logical choice: Trump International Hotel.

We set off to party with other MAGA team members, but were sadly thwarted by red rope and a hotel at capacity. Trump supporters had overwhelmed the property during the course of the evening. On election night, it was the only place to celebrate and we were late to arrive. We tried a few different places afterwards, but nowhere else was partying.

Outside of Trump's hotel, the rest of Washington, DC mourned.

DEPLORABALL

THE DEPLORABALL WAS the hottest ticket in town over inauguration weekend. On January 19th, 2017, over 1,000 deplorables flew in from around the country to rejoice. We were there to celebrate Trump's victory and impending swearing in, but the event symbolized much more. For many of us, the election season had been a time of transformation. We left our old friends and associations behind, we left the Democrats behind, and we embraced a new future. The Deploraball was our first chance to come together as large group and embrace our new community. Being isolated and alone feels terrible and the chance to make new connections was exciting. This event marked the end of one era and the beginning of another. The people who galvanized us online over Twitter, blog posts, and new media now offered a chance to coalesce in real life. The party was sold out and the buzz was on.

The name "Deploraball" was chosen in response to Hillary Clinton's infamous speech where she smeared Trump supporters as racist Nazi scumbags. She said, "You could put half of Trump's supporters into what I call the basket of deplorables. Right? The racist, sexist, homophobic, xenophobic, Islamophobic -- you name it."

Using deplorable to describe ourselves at once deflated the meme and mocked her arrogance. The name was a perfect choice for an inaugural ball meant for the "radical fringe," another one of Clinton's names for us. We weren't going to have a boring party at an empty museum, rubbing shoulders with establishment types, low-level donors, and the stuffy old version of the Republican party. No, this was a night for the new right side of politics, and the edgy name fit. We were the Deplorables and this was our homecoming party.

People traveled from all over the country to celebrate and, in many ways, this party would define our identity moving forward. Though Clinton's gross exaggeration was a political failure, she was right about one thing: under the wide tent of the Trump coalition an undesirable element had snuck in, and it was time to take out the trash. While the vast majority of Trump's supporters denounce racism, oppose bigotry, and welcome people of all kinds, the chaos of the election allowed some bad characters to leverage Trump's popularity into a catalyst of their own. The Deploraball created the moment to purge these true undesirables once and for all.

During the election, the alt-right was somewhat tolerated since they were supporting Trump. Everyone had one common goal: defeat Hillary. But now that the election was over, the new movement needed to enforce its standards and shun the actual Nazis. Trump and his online network of supporters weren't necessarily innocent. During the election, some had cynically accepted the presence of the alt-right. Trump retweeted at least one Twitter account who had posted anti-Semitic things in the past. People had flirted with the alt-right in an effort to gain followers. The war was on to elect Trump and the coalition had to be as big as possible, even if that meant getting dirty for a minute. But this was before the reality of the alt-right was fully understood. For a while, the phrase "alt-right" meant different things to different people.

The alt-right is a loose group of actual racists, neo-Nazis, and hardcore white nationalists. In the turbulence of Trump's jet stream, this group of *real* deplorables had snuck in the back door and publicly supported Trump during the election. In the US, they were led by figures like Richard Spencer, head of the National Policy Institute, a racist organization which tries to hide behind the veneer of calling itself a 'think tank.' In the weeks leading up to the Deploraball, the NPI hosted their annual event in Washington, DC. If attendance at this event was any indicator, Spencer's influence was microscopic. The conference only drew a hundred attendees, but the national media played it up big. Camera crews and journalists documented the event as if it were a major moment in America, despite the pitiful attendance.

This overzealous reporting seemed more effective in creating a useful foil rather than demonstrating journalistic discretion, but both the media and Spencer fed on each other. Spencer got his attention and the media got outrage clicks. And more significantly, the media created a chance to smear all Trump supporters as racists. Propping Spencer up hurt Trump and sold advertising. Spencer and his team didn't disappoint either. During the NPI conference, attendees threw up Hitler salutes and acted like a bunch of Nazis. The media pounced, continuing Hillary's tact of casting all Trump supporters to be as odious as the alt-right. Instead of soberly assessing the true situation, the mass media inflated Spencer's and the alt-right's influence.

I even got caught up for a second. When I first heard "alt-right," I thought it was just a term that bubbled up from the internet, giving a name to people who weren't Democrats or Republicans. To me, the name sounded cool, as if this was the right-leaning conservative group I sought who weren't left over from the old-time establishment. To be alt-right seemed to be alternative, and alternatives to the status quo were exactly what we were after. As a Democrat to Deplorable, I was without a political party and I tried on a few different hats before I found one that fit. I even explored the alt-right personally. I thought for a moment it was going to be my new home.

However, I soon learned there was much more to the alt-right than a catchy name. I learned that they believed in white supremacy. I learned that they hated Jewish people. And I learned that they wanted a white ethno-state in America more than anything else. Appalled, I set out to learn as much as I could in an effort to expose them to the rest of my Democrat to Deplorable travelers. Problem was, when I started asking questions, no one would reply. I reached out the founders of alt-right.com, Richard Spencer, Ramzpaul, and other figureheads. I asked them, "What are your policy positions? What are your plans? What do you wish would happen?" No one would reply with anything concrete. I got empty emails in return or casual dismissals via Twitter. Either they were empty-headed (probably) or ashamed of their stupid ideas (likely), but no one – not even the spokespeople for their group – would engage. Turns out the alt-right was not only stupid, but also cowardly.

To make a clean break from the alt-right and demonstrate who we really were, Richard Spencer and his cronies were banned from the event. The Deploraball organizers prohibited any anti-Semitic or racist behavior, and they issued a blanket ban to keep the trash away from the party. Despite that, there were some rumblings on Twitter of alt-right followers planning to disrupt the event with Nazi salutes. Just in case, I issued a challenge on Twitter, stating that anyone who tried to pull such a stunt would have to face me afterwards.

Promising to meet a Nazi salute with violence was out of character for me, but carving the alt-right away from our Deplorable movement was important. When I landed on this side of the wall, I had to clear out the garbage and underbrush to make way for not only myself, but for all the other people behind me. If it appeared that once you rejected the Democrats all that remained were Nazis in front of you, few more would risk the change. Creating a safe landing space for Democrats and new Deplorables became incredibly important.

I wasn't going to associate with anyone remotely resembling a Nazi. The Deploraball organizers felt the same way. Unfortunately, the rest of the world didn't appreciate the distinctions we tried to make. To them, we were *all* in Hillary's basket of deplorables.

Despite efforts to ban Nazis, Hillary's deplorable smear left an indelible mark. The protests against the event began as soon as the planning for it did. Once the Clarendon Ballroom in Arlington, VA was announced as the initial location, the opposition took immediate action. Protestors flooded the venue with emails, phone calls, and tweets. Despite having a signed contract and a paid deposit, the Ballroom backed out of hosting, fearful that they were opening their doors to actual Nazis rather than ordinary Americans.

With no venue, the event's outcome seemed in jeopardy. It was December, a month before the inauguration would take over the entire city for a week, and most alternatives were already booked. But we found a replacement: Jeff Giesea, one of the event organizers, was once a member at the National Press Club and appealed directly to its executive director. After convincing him that there would be zero tolerance for anti-Semites, neo-Nazis, or the alt-right, the director agreed to host the event. The party was back on.

Just when it seemed the last obstacles had been cleared, the Deploraball was almost sabotaged by a terror attack. A group of violent opposition, known as ANTIFA, plotted to attack attendees with poison gas at the National Press Club. They planned to release toxic chemicals into the HVAC system to burn skin, irritate eyes, and force an evacuation of the building by gassing everyone there. Given that senior citizens and pregnant women were expected to be in attendance, a potential stampede caused by poison gas could have been catastrophic. Luckily, the plot was foiled by the undercover journalism team, Project Veritas. They videotaped the conspirators planning the attack and ANTIFA was ultimately arrested. [16]

Despite protests forcing the Clarendon Ballroom to evict us, despite Nazi's promising to infiltrate us, despite terrorists planning to gas us, my girlfriend and I arrived at the party without a second thought. We were in full party mode, dressed up and ready to meet our new community in person for the first time. All we could think about was our friends, the excitement of the inauguration, and the open bar. This was a celebration and spirits were high. So when we got close to the venue and saw the streets backed up for blocks, we were surprised. Why so much traffic? Why so many street closures? What are all these people doing? What in the world is going on here?

And that's when we saw it... total mayhem. Mobs of people dressed in all black, black hoodies covering their heads and black bandanas covering their faces, piles of garbage on fire. The entire street was filled with 'protestors' convulsing with hatred. Hatred for Trump, hatred for everyone who voted for him, hatred for all the party-goers, and, of course, hatred for alt-right (despite there being none of them around). We tried to make our way to the front door but were pushed back by the mob. "NAZI BITCH!" a woman with purple hair and a nose piercing that made her look like a cow screamed at my girlfriend. "NAZI BITCH! NAZI BITCH! NAZI BITCH!" over and over again in our faces. For a moment we were swallowed up, our noses filled with their stench (yes, you could smell them), and we were jostled as they kept yelling, "NO NAZIS, NO KKK, NO RACIST USA!" over and over again. I held my girlfriend's hand and pushed through the crowd. There was a naked man writhing around. Horns blared in our ears. For a moment it was overwhelming – where in the fuck was the front door?

The journey through the rabble to the Deploraball was a real-life metaphor. We were surrounded by a chaotic mob; they were angry violent people with no regard for reality. They threw batteries at us. They burned MAGA hats. They hated us for being there. They hated us for going to a party. They hated us for being Trump supporters. They threatened us with violence, used intimidation to dissuade us, and literally tried to gas us for our political beliefs. They knew nothing of us personally, they didn't know our names or what we believed. They only knew one thing (and even that was a guess): we were Trump supporters and we weren't human. This was the manifestation of political demagoguery as actual violence. When Hillary called us all deplorables – when she branded us all as racists, when she said we were all homophobic, when she said we all had hate in our hearts – she unleashed the true hatred: the hatred of the left. We weren't the haters but now, the hated. Clinton was truly the chaos candidate, and that moment amidst the mob confirmed it. Politics is ugly business and we were face-to-face with it in the street.

Any hopes I had of a national reconciliation evaporated that night. Hillary didn't create the hatred in our society any more than Trump did, but she did whip it into a frenzy in an effort to win the election. The 2016 election was angry and divisive and reflected the tone of the country. Both sides slashed the other with powerful rhetoric. Hillary called Trump and his supporters misogynists and racists, and Trump fired back by trotting out Bill Clinton's alleged sexual assault victims. The blow-for-blow campaign morphed into actual street violence in 2016 and carried on through the inauguration. The year 2017 would see an escalation into open street battles, regular assaults, and even a death.[17] The mob scene in front of the Deploraball was just a sample of a larger problem, one that would continue to fester as time wore on. The 'protesters' who planned to gas the National Press Club would later become a national story, as the Department of Homeland Security labeled their activities as domestic terrorism.[18] I never expected to confront domestic terror on the way to a party, but this was our new normal. Welcome to the United States in 2017, a nation at war with itself.

About 25 police officers blocked the front entrance to the event. They and their bicycles formed a barrier between the mob and the Deploraball. The police protected us, the reviled Trump deplorables, from the swarming mass of black bloc protesters. My girlfriend and I were dressed in black as well, but our formal party attire separated us from the hoard. A police officer noticed us fighting our way through and said, "Right this way, folks." The barricade opened for a brief moment and we slid through.

At the front door, I turned to take a picture to capture the moment. After a breath, we shook off the bad vibes of the protestors and embraced the light.

Once inside, the energy surrounding us transformed completely. We exchanged angry mobs and their vitriol for an orderly line of festive party-goers. The lobby was bright with high ceilings, allowing us and the rest of the crowd to breathe easier. The stifling mass of people outside provided a stark contrast. The glass facade muted their screams and chants. Genuine warmth and camaraderie filled the lobby. My shoulders relaxed and we took a deep a breath. "Whew!" my girlfriend exhaled as her smile returned. More stunned than anything she reflected, "Well, that's the first time I've ever been called a Nazi!"

Everyone else around us had the same feeling. Folks from all over the country were there to celebrate and the vibes in line were open and welcoming. The security process reminded me of an international flight but none of us minded. There was an ID check, bag check, multiple ticket confirmations, and finally metal detectors. The party was sold out and it took a while to get inside, but no one seemed to care. People were joking about what we'd all just endured, "Hey are you a Nazi? Are you a Nazi? I'm not a Nazi, are you? Where are the Nazis? No Nazis here?" We all shared a laugh. Then we went through the lobby, up the elevator to the 11th floor, and into the party. We were finally at the Deploraball.

I

THE FIRST THING we saw was a man dressed in a suit made entirely of the American flag. There was a Donald Trump impersonator holding court. Middle-aged men in white tuxedo jackets escorted their wives in sequined gowns. Young couples held hands and mingled. The National Press Club has a distinguished history of hosting high-profile events, and now it was our turn for history.

Ross Perot and Jimmy Carter announced their Presidential campaigns at the club. Eisenhower announced his resignation as Army Chief of Staff. Martin Luther King Jr. was the first African American to address the membership. Fidel Castro and Louis Farrakhan, Muhammed Ali and Ken Norton, John F. Kennedy and Nikita Khrushchev... they all walked the rooms before us. Portraits and pictures celebrating the hall's history adorned every wall. There was no avoiding the prominence of the Club and the symbolism of us sharing the same space. We were partying at a venue that once denied Italian fascist Benito Mussolini admittance – if they let us in, we can't be that bad right? Where Teddy Roosevelt once bragged about his big game hunting, where Woodrow Wilson took refuge from the swamp of DC, where Harry Truman once played the piano while serenading Lauren Becall, where Golda Meir, Boris Yeltsin, Nelson Mandela, Ronald Regan, and even the Dalai Lama once held court, us Deplorables now celebrated the imminent presidency of one Donald J. Trump.

The National Press Club bar was the first to reopen in DC after Roosevelt repealed prohibition, so it was no surprise the drinks were flowing. Music played and the energy swelled.

I grabbed my girlfriend's hand and we moved around the room. The event was filled with personalities from the new Trump media universe. The Deploraball was where I first met Jack Posobiec and Gavin McInnes. I saw Laura Southern, Sheriff Clark, and Jim Hoft. But the most notable attendee was Peter Thiel, the founder of PayPal and

Facebook board member. He was the most prominent Silicon Valley leader to back Trump. If Thiel supported Trump, then surely Trumpism wasn't just about pussy grabbing and racial slurs. What did Thiel see that other businessmen didn't? Despite his public support for Trump the candidate, I was stunned he actually attended. I later learned he was connected to the Deploraball through Giesea, as Jeff had worked for Thiel Capital years before. No doubt about it, the Deploraball was the place to be on inauguration weekend.

That's when my night and my life took an unexpected turn. As we stood there soaking in the atmosphere, people started coming up to me. "Are you Jack Murphy?" I was startled; it was the first time I'd ever been recognized in public. At that point in January, I had built a modest Twitter following and my blog was still growing, but I had consistently written and tweeted for months leading up to the election. People were actually paying attention! "I love your work, keep it up!" "It's so great to meet you, Jack!" "Thank you for all you do." After I finished talking with one person, I'd turn my head and there'd be another waiting to say, "Hi!" I was a little embarrassed. And flattered. Writing was just a hobby for me at that point, but the positive feedback from my fellow deplorables was a gift. The encouragement I found at the party led directly to the words on this page.

My transformation from Democrat to Deplorable was nearing completion. I'd deleted my old Democrat associations and embraced the new deplorable world before me. Entering the Deploraball was like entering a new universe, complete with new friends, new opportunities, and a new way of life. It felt like home.

The music stopped and the crowd moved into the main hall as a roster of deplorables addressed the crowd. While the victory speeches were fun, the most memorable ones hinted at a new era in politics and media. The election spawned a new media ecosystem that supported Trump and battled back against the Democrats and the lefty press. Trump took the war directly to CNN with his Fake News campaign, and the new media followed suit. Trump opened a figurative door for a new press landscape to emerge, and then opened a literal one when Lucian Wintrich from the Gateway Pundit became an official White House correspondent. Lucian announced the move to the crowd of deplorables and everyone loved it. He was invading the sacred territory of the snobby establishment media: the White House Briefing Room. Wintrich landing in the White House felt like legitimacy for the new media. It was a significant moment. It was the first time a "blogger" had the same access to the White House as CNN.

But the most significant speech of the night belonged to Jeff Giesea. His speech that night did two things. First, Jeff put words to feelings, relating what it was like to lose friends or be alienated for supporting Trump... something we all had felt. After he brought us together emotionally, he then outlined a vision for the future: the beginnings of a new political philosophy, separate from the establishment Republicans and wildly different than the Democrats. I think his speech was really important so I included the entire text here:

> Hi everyone. My name is Jeff Giesea. Like many of you, I'm a political outsider. To me, the Republican party of Paul Ryan has always felt weak and out of touch, and my libertarian leanings have seemed less and less

relevant in a changing world. It seemed pointless to get involved in elections.

Then Trump came along. A courageous leader who isn't afraid to take on the establishment. An opportunity for fresh approaches to the challenges of our day. An opening to disrupt the GOP and introduce a new type of Republican.

This is what we are here to celebrate tonight -- a new type of Republican and a new movement of Trumpism.

This is a movement. We all know it. We all feel it. And it's not just limited to America.

Many of you worked hard to help elect Trump. If you're like me, it's been an incredible, dramatic, and sometimes traumatic experience. We've been screamed at, unfriended on Facebook, disinvited from dinner parties, and called illiterate.

Many times, I've had to ask myself: Has our world gone completely mad? Consider the people who called us racist simply for wanting to enforce our borders. Or the media that tried to convince us that Michelle Fields was actually assaulted. Or the special needs kid who was tortured on Facebook live and made to drink toilet water because he was a white Trump supporter. Or the protesters outside who planned an acid attack on this party and threw batteries and smoke bombs at you all tonight as you entered. Who are the fascists again?

We the deplorables are here to say ENOUGH. Enough of this liberalism gone wild. Enough of this assault on common sense.

You and everyone in this room is part of something new not just for America but for the world. Since the end of the Cold War, there's been only one option for Western countries: liberal universalism -- or what I call "Davos liberalism."

In recent years we've seen the contradictions of this liberalism. Liberalism, it might be said, is eating itself.

Nowhere is this more obvious than with the migrant crisis in Europe -- where open borders policies are hampering gay rights, women's rights, and the very identities of these nations.

We feel this in America too. Taken too far, the excesses of political correctness and globalism are leading to social fragmentation, growing inequality, and an almost Maoist sense of social justice sanctimony.

We – and the rest of the West – need an alternative to navigate the challenges of the 21st century. We need an alternative that is practical, moral, and common sense.

Trumpism, in my humble view, is that alternative. Trumpism is the way to preserve our civilization while embracing the future. Trumpism, as I see it, is based on three core principles:

Sovereignty – by this I mean secure borders, self-determination, and a stronger sense of national identity and shared values.

Economic nationalism -- in particular a focus on making life better for the middle and working Americans, not just the top 1%.

America first -- particularly in our foreign policy.

If there's a fourth principle it would be resistance to the excesses of political correctness -- or what many of us refer to as cultural Marxism.

Let's be clear that we do not want Trump to become George W. Bush 2.0. We may agree or disagree on issues like gay marriage and social security reform, but those issues aren't what define us.

A question I often think about is: How can we preserve our civilization in a way that's practical, moral and forward-looking?

I think of my grandmother, who came the US from Mexico as a small child in the 1920s. Her family wanted the opportunity for a better life. They wanted to be Americans.

While my grandmother was crossing the border, my great-grandfather on the other side of my family was presiding over the Bohemian Club in San Francisco. He was president of the Bohemian Grove, a place of privilege and power. He was a fierce advocate of Western Civilization and ideals.

The challenge of the 21st century America is to reconcile these two sides of ourselves -- our Anglo, Western heritage and our immigrant, multi-racial one.

It's kind of awkward and messy, but I believe we can reconcile these forces. And that we can do so in a way that works for all Americans. I don't have all the answers, but I am here to talk.

America, this is our "make it work moment."

We in this room want to be constructive. Our hearts our full. We are not going away. We are determined to make America great again for all Americans.

We are the deplorables. Thank you.

The crowd erupted as he finished. His vision echoed my own motivation to support Donald Trump, and based on the crowd's response, Jeff captured our collective ideas. We voted for Trump not because he was a Republican, but in spite of it. We voted for Donald Trump because the Democrats had lost their minds and because the Republicans had turned on the American people in favor of corporate interests and the 1%. The combination of economic Nationalism, Sovereignty, and America First in all things represented a new way forward that accurately reflected the modern times. Forget the Democrats, forget the Republicans, forget the old right, we are the New Right. The Deploraball was our celebration. The event was both a homecoming and a coming-out.

II

WHEN THE DEPLORABALL ended at 11 or 12, the party was hardly over. We spilled out of the Press Club, across the street, and into Shelly's Cigar Bar. Shelly's would later become a sort of social headquarters for the new right media in DC, since the owners didn't mind our politics. Few places in DC are accepting of MAGA folks doing their thing, and that night became the first of several parties to be held there. Spirits were high; not only had we won the election but the party was a smash hit. Mike Cernovich, one of the party planners, sat in a leather chair smoking a cigar, as people took turns approaching to congratulate him. Jim Hoft and Bill Mitchell circulated. All the players from the new media scene were there pressing the party on into the morning.

And that's when fate delivered me a chance to continue my efforts to help purge the alt-right from the new right. Richard Spencer crashed the after-party despite being banned from the main event, openly shunned, and thoroughly unwanted. I had spent the past several months writing about how the alt-right was all wrong, and I wanted Richard to answer some questions. Combined with my earlier warning about anyone pulling any Nazi stunts, this seemed like the perfect chance to get some answers or maybe even have a little confrontation. If Spencer was going show his face at all, I wanted the story to be "Spencer unwanted by Deplorables" rather than have his attendance simply noted or promoted. Knowing the national media was in the room, I set out to make my position clear.

I wanted a confrontation. I was hoping Spencer would push me or take a swing so I could have reasonable cause to pummel him. I badgered him with questions about his idea of a white ethno state and what his vision for the future looked like, but he had no answers. At one point, he just waved his soft hands in the air and said, "History has a way of working these things out."

Spencer offered lame answers and I still hadn't caused a scene, so I kept on. Finally, Richard snapped and started screaming at me. His face was red and he lashed out as he lost control. The moment I wanted was right there – I was about to get into fight with Richard Spencer at the Deploraball after-party. He kept screaming in my face and it was on… until Mike Cernovich stepped in between us and asked me to stand down. Even though I didn't get what I wanted right there, I did succeed at injecting the idea of an alt-right banishment into the narrative.

The next day, *The Atlantic* and *Business Insider* reported on our "fractious" evening, and *The New Yorker* would later run a story outlining the schism.[1920] We'd cleared the trash out and left Spencer and the alt-right all alone. The Deploraball was a huge success as a party, a celebration, and as a tool for marginalizing the alt-right from Trump supporters. It was the right thing to do morally, and optically. I refuse to associate with people like that, and I couldn't stand by and let them infect what was now my new home.

I didn't know it then, but the Deploraball, the people I met there, and the encounter with Spencer lead directly to this book. It was the night I met Jack Posobiec, Jeff Giesea, and many others who formed the core of the movement, the New Right. It positioned me within the emerging new media universe and added to my building credibility as a writer and a thinker.

My beef with Spencer prompted another online personality, Ivan Throne, to propose a debate between me and the alt-right leader. Spencer naturally declined, as he continued to avoid both intellectual and physical confrontations with me, but another prominent thinker in the space stepped up. Vox Day, a controversial author and publisher who is known for his 16 points describing the alt-right, agreed to debate me in Spencer's place. After the recording was finished he asked if I was working on a book, as he might be interested in publishing it. I pitched him on a couple of ideas but as soon as I said, "Democrat to Deplorable," his interested piqued. "That's a great title. You should write that book and send it to us when it's ready." I was a little surprised, and kind of flattered. Even though

Vox and I disagreed often, he respected my thinking and writing well enough to encourage me to write. That was the moment Democrat to Deplorable became real. I'd gone from being a Democrat, into the unknown, landing in the basket of Deplorables, and going from an outsider to part of the movement.

Encouraged by readers I met at the Deploraball, energized by the rousing success of the night, and tantalized with the prospect of publishing my first full length book, I set out to document the experiences I and many others had during the run up to the 2016 election. I knew I wasn't alone in my time in the wilderness. I knew the Democrats pushed many other people away from their home and into the darkness of isolation. But I was the lucky one: I endured the shame, loss of friendships, and the label of racist Nazi to find my new tribe. The Deplorables welcomed me and we had just celebrated our victory. From then on, in February 2017, I went full speed ahead into this new journey, reaching out to hundreds of people across the country, hearing their stories, and working to unearth the forces which rocked our nation on its way to the historic election of Donald Trump. Democrat to Deplorable was born, and I was off and running.

Section Two

The Project

HOW MANY
OF US ARE THERE?

T HE DEPLORABALL SHOWED me I wasn't alone. I found like-minded people after being pushed into the political wilderness. I lost relationships with friends and family members, and I lost the only political party and identity I'd ever known. But the Deploraball taught me there were many more who experienced the same sense of loss I did when the Democrats veered into hysterics and cult thinking and began their excommunication of non-believers. These were the people I wanted to meet. These were the stories I wanted to hear and share. I wanted to bring an authentic and empathetic light to people who had been unfairly maligned. If I could reveal their humanity, maybe I could help bridge the divide between red and blue America.

This book has several goals. Primarily, I want to explain what propelled former Democrats to ditch their tribe and find a new one. This book is a cultural analysis of how and why our country got to this point, where millions of people left the Left and embraced a new version of the Republican party.

As an introduction, I explored my personal journey as a way to divulge the context in which I wrote the book. I did this because understanding the world in which the argument-maker exists is critical to understanding any thesis.

I have my own biases, naturally, but my perspective was born of the circumstances which also motivated millions of others to make the same decision I did. My personal story is a relevant example of the Democrat to Deplorable phenomenon.

I also want this book to be a sort of guide, like a "Lonely Planet" for Democrat to Deplorable voters. People like us, especially those in blue states and cities, endured an arduous path to come out as Trump supporters. The process of changing political parties is unnerving. Fleeing one tribe to join another is unsettling and scary. Leaving behind familial connections to confront the unknown is a bold and challenging adventure. It's a brave step to drop the comfortable narratives which define group membership. Learning the new stories, adopting new group mythologies, and immersing yourself in a new language is hard. It's a long road with no sign posts. It's dark out, your headlights are broken, and you can only see a few feet in front of you. You could veer off the road and into a ditch at any moment. You don't know how long you've been driving and you don't know where the next stop is. If only you had a map. If only there was a friend riding shotgun who could say, "Oh, I've been here before, no worries. Home is just around the next corner."

That's the intention of this book. It's a friend saying you're ok and you're on the right path. It's encouragement to keep going, even if the situation appears bleak. It's a collection of stories and ideas that make you say, *Yes! Finally someone understands me.*

My story alone isn't enough to carve out a space amidst the sea of uncertainty for Democrat to Deplorable voters. Millions of others made the same decision I did, and to unearth a deeper understanding of the cultural energy which exploded into a Trump presidency, I had to reach out to individuals and find their stories. I had to weave each isolated strand into a larger mythology, creating something resilient and powerful, something capable of shielding us from the storm and providing the foundation to support massive cultural change. And to those yet to make the journey, I wanted to leave a roadmap to follow so they could drive straight into town instead of fumbling in the darkness and the unknown.

The first step was to confirm how many Democrat to Deplorable voters there were. Around the time of the election, the media treated the notion of a one-time Barack Obama voter turning on the Democrats to vote for Trump as preposterous. This transition was impossible because, to the media, all Trump voters were simply racists... and racists don't vote for black presidential candidates, do they? If Democrat to Deplorable voters really existed, it would complicate this divisive and simplistic narrative. I knew we were out there, people who had the intellectual and emotional capability to vote both for Obama and for Trump, as contradictory as that may seem. But the media wouldn't reveal our presence in America. They denied our very existence. However, the surveys and polling data began to tell the story and our numbers were even greater than I expected.

Rasmussen Reports analyzed three different polls to estimate the number of Obama-Trump voters. The results they reported were astounding. When I first set out on this project, I figured maybe a million people made the switch, but Rasmussen estimates, "The raw number of such Obama-Trump voters ranges from about 6.7 million to 9.2 million." They caveat their findings by saying voter information is unreliable and that people have a tendency to forget who they voted for (yeah, right), but the numbers blare out the truth. Not only do we exist, but there are literally millions of us across the country.[21]

Six to nine million people! This means that 11-15% of Trump's total votes came from people who once voted Obama. I knew there had to be others like me, but the real numbers blew my mind. Six to nine million people who proudly stood in line to support Barack Obama now fought their way through accusations of racism, sexism, and jingoism to put Trump into office.

The election was decided by 77,000 people across Ohio, Pennsylvania, and Michigan, where just 10,000 votes tipped the election for Trump. The swing states swung and the marginal voter made all the difference. And because OH, PA, and MI flipped from Obama in 2012 to Trump in 2016, it's safe to assume a significant number of the nine million Obama-Trump voters came from these three states and others like them. Based on these numbers, the Democrat to Deplorable voter may be the most powerful voting bloc in America, and there can be little doubt of their contribution to the election of Donald Trump.

I knew Democrat to Deplorable voters were important but now the data confirmed it. Learning all I could about these brave people was not just relevant to me, but now it was also relevant to the study of politics and history at large. It became imperative to document this phenomenon with an open mind and an insider's perspective. Writers and analysts may try to explain how or why nine million people ditched the Democrats, but most couldn't do it fairly. It's too easy to cast all Trump voters as despicable. An honest assessment, free from bias and the whims of corporate-owned editorial boards, would be hard to come by. I figured that mainstream writers would view the D2D voter with disdain, or discard them as racists unworthy of deeper exploration. If the media reports after the election were any indication, my suspicions were correct. Check out some of these headlines:

"Racism Motivated Trump Voters More than Authoritarianism"

- Washington Post

"Economic Anxiety Didn't Make People Vote Trump, Racism Did"

- The Nation

"There's No Such Thing as a Trump Democrat"

- Washington Post

"New Surveys Help Democrats Explain Trump's win: Yes, his Voters are Racist."

- The National Review

"Yes, it Really was Blatant Racism that Gave Us President Donald Trump"

- Salon

Headlines like these were plastered across major media outlets for months after the election. They were written by bitter defeated analysts who had predicted a certain victory for Clinton. The writers were trapped, forced to confront both their fallibility and a challenge to their worldview. They failed to accurately read the nation's mood and to foresee a Trump victory, leaving the pundits' egos in charge of their analysis. Whatever they wrote had to justify their enormous defeat and attack the victorious. There was no way they could provide a rational, reasoned, or, God forbid, a sympathetic justification for the Obama-Trump voter.

It became clear to me that without an insider giving a careful consideration to the Democrat exodus, we were going to be described as a hateful aberration rather than the herald of a new movement. Being cast aside as bigoted racists before and after the election mirrored the reasons why we voted for Trump in the first place. Someone needed to take a deeper look at what really motivated Democrat to Deplorable voters. I demand it. These voters demand it. And quite seriously, history demands it.

THE SURVEY

IT WAS EARLY spring 2017. The afterglow of the Deploraball was fading and I had promised to do something I'd never done: write a book. Frankly, I was a little overwhelmed. I'd written dozens of blog posts and essays, but creating a book out of thin air was a new challenge. I spent weeks brainstorming topics and subjects, structures and narratives, and really just what in the hell to actually write. I converted my dining room into an office and draped the walls with huge pieces of white paper where I spilled my thoughts. I even replaced the picture on the wall with the biggest white board I could find. Aesthetics took a back seat to practical realities and my stormy brain exploded into the room.

I settled on a plan after several starts and stops, periods of inspired work mixed with weeks of dreaded writer's block. I wanted to tell my story, the detailed accounts of several others like me, and buttress those with data from a national survey. And when that was finished, I would wrap the book up with what I was calling the "Big Finish," a series of essays which put everything into context. Me>the stories>the survey>the big finish. The idea was to build concentric circles of information, beginning with myself in the middle and then expanding to include larger groups of people, additional data and information, and finally the big picture.

I started with the survey. I created an online questionnaire of 67 questions. Some were multiple choice, some asked whether people agreed or disagreed with a statement, and others were open-ended, asking folks to provide responses in their own words. It was long and ambitious. I wondered if people would finish it.

My goal was to learn about these voters directly. I wanted them to have a chance to say what they wanted to say, however they wanted to say it. There had been a number of articles written based on the National Election Commission data set, but I didn't think that survey asked the right questions. It seemed like both the analysis and the NEC data itself was designed in such a way to make all Trump voters appear racist. They take questions which could be read a few different ways and infer racism in the answers. It's a roundabout approach intended to discover latent racism, because it's believed people hide their true feelings when answering direct questions. The assumption is that a respondent's hidden racism can be revealed through indirect methods. Basically, they use trick questions to unearth hidden motivations. This leaves interpretation up to the reviewers, where they get to put words in people's mouths and declare you to be something you're not. That was something I wanted to avoid. So I made my own.

Reader response to my survery exceeded all of my expectations. I promoted the survey on my blog and on Twitter. Over 1,300 people answered some portion of the survey, and 56% of them completed it. The high completion rate surprised me given the length of the questionnaire. The data shows that some people spent 45 minutes or more to complete it. People put a lot of energy into their responses, and many thanked me for giving them a chance to be heard. In a world that refuses to acknowledge their existence, Democrat to Deplorable voters were thrilled to finally have a voice outside of the ballot box.

The survey had 15 open-ended questions where people left a short answer response. Some people chose to write a short phrase, but many wrote entire paragraphs. I have over 15,000 open-ended replies from the entire survey set. The volume of information was overwhelming. And while it's hard to make generalizations from open-ended answers, they did provide me with a vast trove of comments from people all over the country. Reading them gave me a sense of the feelings and tone of the Democrat to Deplorable voter. I use some of these quotes throughout the book to offer another voice in support of my assertions.

I

THERE ARE MANY possible critiques of my questionnaire and I want to them address them head-on. First, you could dismiss my findings by saying the respondents were a self-selected group of people who already shared my views. This may be true, but I don't think it really matters. The population I wanted to research is a particular set of people who chose to vote Trump after Obama. Reaching out to them directly is logical. There was no need to survey Hillary voters and those who opposed Trump. I wanted answers from this exact group of people, so I went right to them.

Other credible surveys are subject to similar criticism. A huge amount of what passes for scientific research is conducted on freshman psychology students at universities. This is just another self-selected group of people. If you have a problem with my survey population but don't care that "science" is using a group of 18-year-olds in college to generalize about human populations, you're welcome to stop reading now.

Another critique of the survey is that many non-Democrats responded. Somehow, people misread the introduction where I explained that the survey was about Democrat to Deplorable voters, not Republicans in general. This phenomenon inflated the number, but I solved this problem easily enough. For my final analysis I filtered the respondents down to just the people who agreed with the following statement: "I once supported the Democrats but now I support Donald Trump." In total, 504 people answered affirmatively and they became my final data set.

Finally, one could argue that I didn't get a representative sample of Democrat to Deplorable voters because I used the internet to distribute and administer the questionnaire. I tweeted out the survey, posted it to Facebook and elsewhere, and every single person who answered it did so online. In the old days this approach may have missed certain populations, but basically everyone is online today in some form or another. When traditional surveys rely on phone calls or paid respondents, they encounter their own set of biases. Pollsters are not reaching younger voters when they rely on landlines. Who even has a landline today? Perhaps some Democrat to Deplorable voters are not active online. Perhaps some of them aren't inclined to use Facebook or Twitter or visit the websites that linked to my survey. It's possible. So a fair critique is that my data set skewed towards online users. I'm ok with that.

I wanted the survey answers to help tell the story I wanted to share, to confirm my own suspicions and put words to feelings. Sure, it may be confirming my own viewpoint going in, but there is value to that. I can confidently make generalizations of Democrat to Deplorable voters who use the internet, and that's a lot of people. Millions of them, in fact. And since the election was decided by 77,000 voters in states that flipped from blue to red, the survey data remains relevant in spite of this critique.

So, here it is. In the Appendix you'll find the basic demographic data of the 504 Democrat to Deplorable voters who made the final data set. I've sprinkled quotes and data from the survey throughout the book and they all come from this set of respondents, unless otherwise noted.

THE PEOPLE

I HAD TO GET out there. I wanted to absorb the energy of the American people. I needed to see the looks in their eyes. I had to read their body language. If they felt disempowered, I wanted to hear their desperation. If they felt angry, I wanted to see their rage. If they were excited, I wanted their energy to rub off on me and into this book. There was no other way to accomplish my goals without leaving my dining room in Washington, DC.

So my girlfriend and I hopped in my Ford Explorer and set out exploring, armed with little more than empathy, understanding, and a pocket voice recorder. We drove through western and northern Maryland, into the hills and mountains of southern Pennsylvania, and up to the far northeastern corner of the state. We drove through suburban sprawl, the endless replication of grocery-anchored shopping centers and their satellite fast-food places. We passed by decaying factories, their red-orange rust contrasting sharply against the blue sky. We stumbled onto cross country trucking routes, industrial parks, forgotten towns, and thriving cities. We stopped at diners, farmer's markets, restaurants, shopping malls, food courts, taverns, and pubs. We walked through small towns, stopping strangers on the street and interviewing shopkeepers. We approached people sitting on park benches or saddled up to the bar for a pint. We talked to just about anyone who would entertain us and I was continually amazed at how open people were. They wanted to tell their stories and I wanted to listen.

We had countless conversations with voters, far too many to share in the book. There was the young gay couple at a corner pub on St. Patrick's Day who ranted about immigration and guns. There was the Serbian immigrant having dinner with her American husband, who wanted lower taxes and more job opportunities. There was the single dad with his daughter who loathed what Trump said about women. There was the blond woman with her husband who said feminism was the root of all evil. There was the Indian immigrant in his late 60s working the late shift at a small-town motel. A lacrosse team. Retired firefighters. Lawyers. District Attorneys. College kids. From the diner waitress to the art gallery manager, from the fruit stand operator to the international business owner, we talked with more people and heard more stories than I can share. Though not all of them made it into print, each experience informed me as I wrote the book.

I engaged with America outside of my blue bubble and was reminded of what an aberration Washington, DC is compared to the rest of America. DC is 90% Democrat. Most of America is not. And swing states like PA and OH certainly are not. From the first conversation I had at a greasy spoon in a small town in southern Pennsylvania, I knew my decision to hit the road was a great idea.

The authentic energy generated from these conversations was exactly what I was after. The 2016 election was emotional, it was angry, it was exhausting – and I discovered that once they became comfortable, people had pent-up thoughts and emotions ready to burst out of their cautious minds and into the air between us. This is what I wanted. I wanted to feel their emotions myself. I wanted to share in their joy or anger. More than anything, I wanted to understand them. At times, I felt more like a therapist than a journalist, just nodding and encouraging people to share. It was cathartic. They needed me as much as I needed them. The good conversations were shared experiences which I will never forget. And some of the best ones made their way into this book.

I

BUT DRIVING AROUND was only going to get me so far. I had to hear from more people than just those within a few days drive from my house. So I put out an open call for interviews. I offered my ear to any Democrat to Deplorable who wanted to share their story. With a blog post, a few tweets, and a public calendar, I was able to line up more interviews than I could manage. I set up a mini recording studio to record our conversations and sat down in my dining room once again to hear what America had to say.

I recorded about 50 hours of Skype calls over the course of three months. Some calls lasted two hours or more and I had follow up conversations with many people. I spent days reviewing them, listening over and over, noting key passages, copying quotes down word-for-word, trying to parse together these people's life stories from just a few hours of discussion. Ultimately, this format was more useful than random street conversations. Though I did follow up with people I met on my travels, having the chance for a thorough interview gave me the best insights. Two of the most in-depth chapters of this book were researched using Skype calls like this.

Between the survey, my road trips, and interviews, I heard from upwards of 1,500 people. I had innumerable in-person conversations, I recorded a work weeks' worth of interviews, and I read over 10,000 short answer responses from my survey. I did all this because when I set out to write this book, I knew I needed more than just my story and opinions. And I couldn't rely on other people's investigations or I'd just be writing a book report. So I conducted original research across media, locations, and techniques. I distilled what I heard into themes and analyzed the data for trends. And best of all, I heard the true stories of American voters who braved the unknown, ditched the Democrats, and embraced Donald Trump.

So, now you know me, my story, and my goals for the project. What follows is the result of my life experience, a year's worth of work, and the open honesty of the people I talked to. Without further ado, I present to you, The Deplorables.

GREG

G REG WAS RAISED in the Lehigh Valley area of Pennsylvania. His fellow high school students were the sons and daughters of farmers, tradesmen, and factory workers. The middle class American dream, where getting ahead meant working hard and providing for your family, once defined the spirit of his hometown in rural Pennsylvania. But as the mills closed and the factories departed for NAFTA-inspired foreign shores, the once-stable middle-class area felt less like the land of opportunity and more like the field of broken dreams.

Union life defined the men of his family. Greg's father is a cop and his stepdad was a unionized telecommunications technician. Blue collar was a term that bothered neither of them, and hard work brought both the daily satisfaction of a job well done as well as the daily bread. To say Greg's childhood was working class is no slight. These men are the heart and soul of the American economy and our way of life. Fortunately for Greg, he and his immediate family were spared when the recessions and trade wars hit. But for those around him, many weren't as lucky.

Plants and factories have been closing all over the Lehigh Valley for years, and the latest news hit right before election day: Kraft Heinz announced on November 2nd, 2016 that they'd be closing yet another major manufacturing center. The global corporation abandoned almost 500 jobs after nearly 40 years in Pennsylvania. The long-time workers received their layoff notice just weeks before

Thanksgiving, dampening plans for family celebrations and reunions. What could be more stressful entering the holiday season than learning your corporate bosses cancelled your paycheck in the name of higher profits and greater efficiencies?

Sadly for the Lehigh Valley, this was a common occurrence. Bethlehem Steel closed in 1995 and since then, countless other jobs said their final goodbyes, giving a cold hard truth to the name 'Rust Belt.' When your home is described as a decaying, abandoned, empty shell of something which was once great, it's no challenge to consider how this affects the psyche of a community. Globalism snatched their pride and replaced it with a gnawing sense of obsolescence. While it's true some new industries have created jobs in the Lehigh Valley, they often pay less, require more hours, or demand specialties that the typical resident doesn't have. A golden era ended and an uncertain fog settled over many of Greg's friends and family.

So, when Donald Trump came along with a promise to Make America Great Again, his message struck true. The sense of fear and loss of those abandoned by their employers was palpable throughout the region. Many families had to move to find better opportunities, disrupting their children's lives by withdrawing them from high school mid-year. The community was dwindling and the layoffs eroded their former vision of home.

I

THE LEHIGH VALLEY is made up of three counties in Pennsylvania: Carbon, Lehigh, and Northampton. Each county voted unanimously for Bill Clinton in '92 and '96, as well as for Al Gore in '00. All three voted for Barack

Obama in '08. In fact, this region was completely blue for 25 years except for Carbon County in '04 and '12. But the Democrats' grip on the region faded over time as the realities of NAFTA and impact of global trade became too powerful to ignore. Greg told me his family looks back to the 1990s as a turning point. Bill Clinton signed NAFTA and the people of the Lehigh Valley blamed him for eviscerating their way of life. As the American Dream turned to dust and slipped through their fingers, Pennsylvanians blamed the Democrats who had "sold them out." Greg's family had enough of Bill Clinton's NAFTA and turned towards the one place they'd find a comforting voice: Fox News.

Greg's grandparents and their friends watched Fox News every day. He recalls it being on every time he went to their houses, or at stores, or anywhere there was a TV. No matter the occasion, Fox News was there to bleat on about Bill Clinton, the Democrats, and anyone else the conservative media outlet decided to attack that day. This was a big deal considering that Greg's family were union people and life-long Democrats, but the outlook for the region was bleak and getting even bleaker. Someone had to take the blame, and to many, the Democrats were the fall guys.

While some people in the Lehigh Valley found solace in television news, Greg himself wasn't satisfied.

"Eventually, I just got sick and tired of Bush and Fox News. That's when I started being able to research for myself and look into things. That's when I came to Obama in 2008. It was time for something different and Obama promised hope and change. That's what I thought we needed at the time, so I went with it."

Greg's experience mirrored the region's. Their interest in Bush and the Republicans peaked in '04 and by '08, the area returned solidly blue.

Greg cast his first vote in a presidential election for Barack Obama in 2008. He had high expectations and bought into Obama's promise to shake things up. After years of seeing his community stripped apart factory by factory, job by job, Greg welcomed the feeling of optimism and high expectations. Things needed to change and Obama was the change agent of the day.

Not only did Greg hope Obama could help restore the dignity of the working people from his community through economic development and a restoration of meaningful middle-class work, but he also heard Obama's plea for whistleblowers to call out the nefarious elements of the bureaucracy. For Greg, Obama was not only a chance to restore economic strength to the nation and his region, but an opportunity to reduce corruption and waste. Obama seemed to be a champion for him and many others. Greg was not alone, of course, and Obama swept to victory in 2008 with the support of the key swing state of Pennsylvania. So strong was Obama's victory there, so seemingly entrenched was the blue color of the Democrats, that when it came time for Hillary Clinton's campaign in '16, she referred to Pennsylvania as part of her impenetrable "blue wall." But her assumption that PA would easily go her way revealed a deep (and ultimately fatal) miscalculation.

President Obama was once a guy Greg thought he "could sit down and have a beer with." Obama felt authentic, reasonable, and familiar. It was good to send someone like that to Washington, someone who would look out for regular Americans, bring us something to look forward to, and hopefully end the foreign wars in Iraq and Afghanistan.

Like many other Democrat to Deplorable voters, one of Greg's primary issues was ending the American wars abroad. In 2008, the United States had been at war for years, dropping bombs in numerous countries –killing enemy combatants, but also murdering civilians, ruining cities, wasting taxpayer money, and worst of all, sacrificing the lives of our young American soldiers. The very same families affected by factory closures and the industrial recession in Pennsylvania were the ones sending their sons and nephews to fight on the other side of the world. For Greg, the bombs had dropped long enough and it was time for peace.

Many of us were war-fatigued at that time. The benefits to the United States were hard to quantify, while the expense in lives and treasure were bold and clear. The middle east wars were George W. Bush's legacy and an ongoing reminder of his ineptitude. He proudly declared "Mission Accomplished" in 2003, yet by the election in 2008, the thousands of troops on the ground said otherwise. The war felt like a mistake, there were no weapons of mass destruction after all, yet it persisted. For voters who preferred a 'live and let live' approach in both politics and foreign policy, Obama, not John McCain, was the only choice.

But Obama continued the wars in Afghanistan and Iraq and even expanded his target list. In his final year in office, Obama bombed Syria, Yemen, Libya, Somalia, and Pakistan as well. All told, he dropped 26,171 bombs that year.[22] Even more troubling, Obama expanded the drone assassination program, using a robot army in the sky to attack 10 times as many people as Bush had.[23] In the eyes of many of his own supporters, Obama evolved from a harbinger of hope to a great world-wide menace. Rather than bring peace to the United States and the world, Obama rained bombs on more countries and people than before. The Americans who believed Obama would restore humanity and sanity to the highest office after George W. Bush's failures reached their breaking point.

If jobs weren't coming back to Pennsylvania and the bombs still fell on the middle east, then the promises of the Obama campaign turned out to be nothing more than empty lies. When Hillary Clinton pitched herself as the extension of Obama's policies for another four years, she made a cataclysmic error. Why would the people of Pennsylvania want more of the same when the same meant fewer jobs and more war?

The post-mortem on Obama's presidency started to become clear in the spring of 2017. Where Obama was once the shining new face of the Democrats and the leader of a great coalition, Hillary Clinton and her team now blame her loss on what could be called a failed presidency.[24] After all, if eight years of Obama gave birth to a Trump administration, what value was he to the Democrats? Had Obama followed through on his promises and not forgotten the people of Pennsylvania, maybe Hillary Clinton would be president today. Or so their thinking goes.

For Democrat to Deplorable voters, this disenchantment with Obama was one reason we were open to something new. Hillary Clinton, all of her own problems aside, promising to give us more of the same seemed like a vote for the status quo... and the status quo wasn't good. Worse, her confrontational approach to Russia over Syria highlighted a stark contrast between her and Trump. While Trump shared his preference for good relations with Putin and the Russians, Clinton promised conflict.

Clinton's policy prescription of a no-fly zone in Syria presented Democrat to Deplorable voters with a dilemma. Sticking with the Democrats and supporting Hillary seemed like a surefire way to increase global conflict rather than mitigate it. Just like in 2008, the Democrat to Deplorable voter wanted peace over war. Shockingly enough, Trump – who boasted he was the most "militaristic one of all" at one point – became the peace candidate, and Hillary become the war-monger. Trump promised to get us out of Syria and Clinton wanted to escalate, even if that meant a confrontation with Putin. Syria and the Middle East seemed like a bad reason to go to war with Russia, and besides, none of us believed the news that was coming out of Syria anyway.

ISIS and Islamic terrorism are the immediate threats. In a world where religion and ethnicity define the combatants, why would Americans want to fight Russia? After all, they face risks from ISIS and terrorism just like we do. They should be our natural ally in the war against Islamic terrorism, not our enemy of the day. Democrat to Deplorable voters saw through the noise of the Syrian conflict for the real truth. Democrats want war with Russia and Deplorables want peace, while we focus on the real and immediate threats to national security. Progressives may find it difficult to admit, but in 2016, they were the war-mongers and Trump offered the prospect of peace.

Greg, his family, and the people of the Lehigh Valley were exhausted. They were frustrated that the country had been grappling with the same issues for a decade or more. What they wanted was less war and more jobs, but instead they got more bombs and fewer factories. The

Democrats once counted on the Lehigh Valley as a guaranteed win, but their grip on the region had been slipping. And finally, in 2016, the unthinkable happened: two of the three counties, and a majority of the voters, ditched the Democrats and embraced Donald Trump. In a state where the margin of victory was a few thousand votes, this sudden turn to the Republicans made a major impact. Greg's choice to support Donald Trump didn't alienate him from his friends and family like it did for many others because the entire area was with him. After years of lies, betrayals, shuttered factories, and falling bombs, the people of the Lehigh Valley said enough was enough. It was time to Make America Great Again.

SARAH

IN THE LATE 1970s, Sarah's mom, Nancy, decided to become a professional woman. She was a feminist and learned that success meant a secure career separate from her husband's. Full of hope and energy, Nancy enrolled in college wide-eyed at the possibilities. Would she become a doctor? A lawyer? Maybe a university professor? No, something new and different lured her away from the more obvious paths.

While on campus, the Professional Air Traffic Controllers Organization (PATCO) recruited her with offers of a steady salary, secure employment, and a growth industry. Even though she had never dreamed of being an air traffic controller, guiding planes to safety seemed like a safe way to guide her own life towards independence, strength, and the realization of her dreams. As long as Nancy went to college, got good grades, and a good job, she would be able to secure her future happiness. She wasn't alone with this line of thought. More women in the country felt that way as feminism guided young women into putting their career first above everything else. A good job and budding career replaced marriage and family as a woman's first step towards a happy successful life.

Nancy graduated and joined PATCO. Union membership was natural back then. Organized labor was powerful and their public demonstrations of force resonated with the American people. In 1970, five million people went on strike in various industries.[25] In 1974, three million. All told, in the '70s over 20 million people walked out of their jobs and onto the picket lines in hopes of obtaining better wages and improved working conditions. Labor unions represented the working class of America against the capitalists and the government, and over time they made significant changes. Striking workers earned increased salaries, safer workplaces, and common sense labor benefits over large parts of the 20th century. They were a force for good. OSHA, child-labor protections, and a living wage are at least partially a result of their efforts. Factory owners no longer chained exit doors shut or prevented workers from taking breaks. Instead, they now provided fire exits, safety standards, and health insurance. If that seems reasonable to you, thank labor unions.

When Nancy was pregnant with her daughter, Sarah, it was PATCO's turn to strike. On August 3rd, 1981, while seven months pregnant, she joined the picket line to make her statement loud and clear. PATCO and 12,000 union members walked out of their jobs and into a strike, demanding higher wages and a shorter work week. Air traffic control is a notoriously stressful job and the union members were suffering. It was time to take a stand. Unfortunately for Nancy, the loudest and clearest statement of all came just days later, from President Ronald Reagan himself.

Reagan gave PATCO one warning. He said they were violating federal law and would be fired en masse if they did not return to work in 48 hours. The striking workers ignored his threat.

Two days later, the President of the United States fired all 12,000 unionized air traffic controllers in one fell swoop, not only ending their current employment but prohibiting them from ever being hired again in the future.

Nancy's dreams of a stable life, secured by professional unionized work, crumbled around her. The one job she trained for was gone, along with any hopes of ever working in her industry again. Because the Federal Aviation Administration was the only employer for air traffic controllers, Nancy was left pregnant, unemployed, and with no career options or path forward. Her once secure future disintegrated overnight into a terrifying shroud of uncertainty. Imagine what that must be like. One moment you're thinking about your baby's future, proud of the way you've set your family up for success. The next, you're in the wilderness with no job, no career, no training for any other work, and a newborn baby arriving any moment.

All of this thanks to President Ronald Reagan.

It is said that Reagan killed organized labor once and for all on that day in August 1981. Take away a union's power to strike and they have few other effective tools. Breaking the unions favored the capitalists and the government at the expense of the working class in America, and this moment was a major turning point.

Nancy and her family didn't just lose a job that day, they also gained a permanent, life-long affiliation with the Democratic Party who supported them against the Reagan Republicans. Unions were blue and good. Republicans were red and bad. The real world has a way of injecting itself into ideological considerations. Reagan killed Nancy's dreams, broke the unions, and made her a Democrat for life.

Since 1981, the number of strikers per year has dwindled from millions in the 70s to a mere 99,000 in 2016.[26]

This may have been labor's last stand in America, but it was just the beginning for Nancy and her family. Her daughter, Sarah, carried on her mother's blue union affiliation. Today, she is a card-carrying member of the Nevada State Teachers Union and she's as blue as it gets.

Nancy's story shaped Sarah's worldview as an adult. Sarah remembers her mom being "really bitter." Despite doing what she was told (go to college, get a good job), the promised security never came. The economic stress on a young family led to a divorce, several moves, and a gnawing feeling that life would never be as good as it was the day before Reagan broke her union, her stability, and her dreams. Nancy, and eventually Sarah, blamed the GOP for their troubles, engendering a future of activism and kicking off an arc which would take Sarah all the way from the school rooms of Nevada to the floor of the 2016 Democratic National Convention in Philadelphia.

I

SARAH'S OWN DAUGHTER was a micro-preemie. Weighing less than one pound at birth, her survival chances were slim. Despite the long odds, she survived an extended stay in a neonatal unit to join her mother at home. When Sarah looks into her eyes, she knows what a precious gift she has. Each day, Sarah works hard to provide a safe home and to be an outstanding role model. Being a mother and caretaker of children is the focus of her life.

Sarah teaches disadvantaged middle school kids in a rough Nevada neighborhood. For nine years she has taught at a Title 1 school, a designation reserved for schools in the poorest areas of the United States. In exchange for federal funding, Title 1 schools agree to adhere to federal stipulations on testing, teacher reviews, compensation, and other measures. Schools feel the long reach of the Department of Education creep all the way from Washington into their individual classrooms. Lawmakers and regulators in the capital make sweeping commandments from on high, and they roll downhill to the teachers and students.

The most infamous legislation of this kind was George Bush's No Child Left Behind Act of 2001 (NCLB), which forced schools to meet standardized testing targets. Like an alien tentacle, NCLB reached across the country and wrapped itself around the autonomy of local educators, strangling their independence and stifling their craft in the name of money and power. NCLB may have brought additional funds to school districts but it also brought a relentless focus on standardized testing, drowning out subjects like art, science, and social studies in the name of test preparation. NCLB perverted the entire system and teachers were incentivized to drop holistic approaches to education under the spectre of financial punishment. Even its eventual replacement, Every Student Succeeds Act (ESSA), failed to relieve the pressure and some teachers stopped teaching anything which couldn't be captured by test scores. The federal government forced local schools into compliance. The lack of autonomy and hyper-focus on metrics not only harmed the kids but it demoralized teachers, turning them into test prep machines and tools of federal policy. To make things worse, teacher compensation was tied to test scores. NCLB and ESSA sucked the life from schools, administrators, and eventually, even from Sarah.

Despite her daughter's health concerns, Sarah decided to get political. She dedicated her free time to the Nevada State Caucus. She is a remarkable public servant, works tirelessly to educate impressionable and needy children, and participates in national elections, all while caring for her young infant daughter. Sarah's disappointment with NCLB was just *that* powerful. She knew it had to be changed. When Barack Obama promised to change this legislation, Sarah supported him in the caucus and voted for him in the national election.

She told me during our interview, "I remember crying watching him accept the nomination. I felt so optimistic about the future." In Obama she saw a young, charismatic leader offering a vision of hope and change so powerful, it lifted her spirits in face of a tireless work schedule and difficult home life. He just had that effect on people. Sarah was not alone. The nation felt the same and it lifted Obama from community organizer to national leader in a few short years. If anyone could fix the way we teach our young children, surely Barack Obama was the man.

"I was so proud to vote for him."

Ultimately, Obama failed to deliver his promised hope and change to education. His point man, Secretary of Education Arne Duncan, drew the ire of Sarah and her union, the National Education Association.[27] Implementation of Common Core standards and a continued obsession with standardized tests was both divisive and a massive failure. But Sarah's unyielding support for the Democrats continued despite her disappointment. Blue union blood runs deep and Sarah's Democratic roots still held strong.

A few years later, when Sarah first heard of Bernie Sanders, she thought he seemed like a good and honest guy. She supported national health care and related to his anti-establishment message. She thought, "If Bernie ever ran for president, I might actually vote for him." So when Sanders announced his candidacy on her daughter's birthday, it struck her as a good omen. Sarah was all in.

Continuing her history of public service, she volunteered for the local county caucus in February 2016.

II

NEVADA'S PROCESS FOR selecting their national nominee for President is unusual. Rather than simply hold state-wide elections, Nevada's caucus process has three distinct parts: 1) a county-level vote, 2) a county-level convention, and 3) a state-level convention. A caucus is an open-call voting system which requires attendance at each session in person and public voting. There are several criticisms of this system. The open call process may subject caucus-go-ers to peer pressure and the large time commitment ex-cludes many voters from the process. Active duty armed service members, those who work all day, or caretakers who can't leave their posts, have difficulty participating. Despite these critiques, the caucus system is thought to at-tract motivated, high-information party members as com-pared to the typical turn out in a simple primary system.

Clark County, Nevada is the state's most influential county, as it has the largest population. The vote in Clark usually decides the state outcome, so the battle for Clark is the battle for Nevada. In February 2016, Hillary Clinton won step #1. But Bernie Sanders won step #2, when far more of his delegates attended the county convention than Hillary's did. The conflict between these two results set up showdown in step #3, the state convention, where the delegates are chosen for the National Democratic Convention in Philadelphia.[28] Clinton's victory in Nevada was dependent upon winning the state convention. So the DNC (which was basically controlled by Clinton) worked to manipulate the outcome through heavy-handed tactics and legal maneuvering. The DNC wanted to make sure Clinton would win Nevada.

Sarah remembers feeling like the entire thing was set up in favor of Hillary. Parking lots close to the venue were suspiciously closed. Visiting delegates scrambled to find far away off-site parking. There was an early quorum call. Some delegates were still stuck outside when registration ended. As a result, not all of them were eligible to vote and people were mad. "It was gnarly," Sarah reflected. State officials even adopted a temporary set of rules which further limited the ability of Sanders' delegates to vote. People shouted out from the floor, "This is fixed!" And to top it off, Democratic party officials colluded with Casino employers to keep Bernie voters from taking the day off to vote.[29]

Nevada State Conventions are always acrimonious, but this one was unusually violent. According to Rolling Stone, delegates threw chairs, made death threats, and the party leadership shut down the convention before its business was concluded. Just weeks before the convention, someone fired bullets into Sanders' campaign headquarters while he was there, and a staffer's apartment home was broken into and ransacked. Politics in Nevada is a rough and tumble business where casino bosses and political operators collude to manipulate votes, where there are Watergate-style break-ins, and where even gunshots are fired at campaign headquarters.

By the time they voted, 58 Sanders delegates had been disqualified and nearly 500 were either unable to register or were mysteriously prevented from attending. All of Clinton's game day tactics had the desired effect. Despite beginning the day with a sizable delegate advantage over Clinton, Sanders still managed to lose the State Convention under protest conditions. Eventually, the police were called to clear out the hall as delegates still raged at each other four hours past the scheduled end time.[30]

Sarah's Democratic loyalties remained true despite the drama. She was selected to represent the Sanders delegation in Philadelphia and decided to attend. "These people were my heroes. Barbara Boxer, Nancy Pelosi, Al Franken. I wanted to go. I figured I'd give it a shot. I'm union and they offered me a stipend." Sarah hoped her experience would be different in Philly, but the nasty tenor which marred the Nevada State Convention followed her across the country. Trust among Democrats deteriorated not only locally, but nationally.

The events in Nevada were backdropped by ongoing reports that the national DNC process was rigged for Clinton. Hillary had taken control of the DNC by funneling donations and colluding with the former Chair of the committee, Debbie Wasserman Schultz, who was forced to resign in disgrace. By the time everyone arrived in Philadelphia, the Democrats were at war with each other and the mood reflected it.

Sarah told me she was shoved, screamed at, poked, prodded, and even stomped on by Hillary supporters at the national convention, leaving her with two broken toes, some bruises, and plenty of resentment. Sarah even saw a woman get shoved down the stairs just for being a Sanders delegate. She described the experience as "pretty brutal."

Hillary's people did not want the Sanders delegates on the convention floor.

"They were mean to us. It sounds childish, but they wanted us to leave so they could fill our seats with fillers. The fill-in people were waiting in a catered tent,

ready to take your seat as soon as you left. They didn't even give the Sanders people a bottle of water."

Sarah knew the Sanders delegation was unwanted.

But they didn't go without a fight. Bernie never released his delegates to vote for Hillary, despite his gracious speech and endorsement. His supporters staged a walk-out to protest Debbie Wasserman Shultz. They wore neon green shirts which stood out in the darkened convention hall, their glowing presence a reminder of the party's disharmony. And they even put up a Jill Stein for President banner as Hillary walked to the stage. At the end of it all, Clinton was forced to use the unbound super delegates to secure the nomination as Sarah and her fellow Sanders delegates refused to give her their votes.

The Democratic National Convention may have given Hillary the nomination but it also split the party. Clinton failed to bring the Sanders people into the fold and many of them abandoned the party afterwards, swearing to never vote for Clinton. Some, like Sarah, went even further, opening their mind to new ideas and new candidates... and even to Donald Trump.

SARAH HAD BEEN a Bernie Sanders delegate, but more than that, she was a willing, excited participant in the electoral process. She volunteered her free time to caucus with the other Democrats, while others worked weekend service jobs in Las Vegas. She gave her time, energy, money, passion... just about everything she had. Except her vote.

Somewhere on the path as union member, public school teacher, and Democratic delegate, Sarah's party abandoned her and shoved her aside. The callous and undemocratic way in which she was silenced ripped an irreparable gash in her blue democratic heart. The way she saw it, Hillary stole the nomination from Bernie Sanders. Once the primaries were over, Sarah had only one thing on her mind: stop Hillary Clinton.

If a lifelong Democrat like Sarah could be trampled by the Clinton machine, if her passion could be extinguished, if her family legacy could be reconsidered, then what does it say about Hillary and her minions? Rather than enlist Sarah in support, rather than respect her at the convention, rather than listen to her voice, Hillary Clinton and her followers literally shoved Sarah aside and forgot about her.

Well, Sarah did not forget. How could she? Sarah confronted the cynicism of the Clinton monarchy and, in the process, lost her idealization of American democracy. She watched Bernie Sanders be subsumed by elite political powers. She heard his populist voice be silenced despite the pleas of the party base and the raucous sounds from the convention floor.

What does it take for a DNC delegate to retreat from the party of her childhood and embrace the pussy-grabber, Donald Trump?

For Sarah, it took a firsthand glimpse at the corruption and dishonesty of Hillary Clinton and the DNC war machine. The broken bones, thousands of dollars wasted, days and weeks of disrespect, and what looked like the middle finger from Barbara Boxer at the Nevada State Convention. She was lied to, manipulated, and shunned by her own people. The betrayal stung. She wasn't sure what was real and what was a lie anymore. Just like her mother 30 years ago, Sarah endured her own PATCO moment, where petty promises shattered under the weight of power and corruption.

As the Democrats told Sarah "Fuck you" with their fingers, she told them the same with her vote. Hillary Clinton killed the Democrat in Sarah and delivered her unto Trump.

But the transformation of Sarah from Democrat to Deplorable didn't stop with a simple vote. The 2016 election sent Sarah on a journey into the political and cultural wilderness where she learned to question sacred truths. Her personal trauma spurred deeper reflection and what she found was tumor ready for treatment. Entering the Deplorable universe brings you into contact with previously hidden communities, ones you kind of knew existed, but as a Democrat, you never seriously considered. Sarah's blue shroud lifted and what she saw changed not just her vote, but her life.

Her story is a common one. When people make the switch from Democrat to Deplorable, they don't do it by happenstance and they certainly don't do it causally. The blue pill is a temporary derangement while the red pill is a permanent new perspective. As one lie falls from its false pedestal, another appears, weakened and ripe for evisceration. Sarah didn't just ditch the Democrats, she opened her mind to perspectives which offered comfort and stability, rather than fear and chaos.

> *"It feels like vertigo. Spiritual vertigo. Everything you thought you were doing right, isn't. It's not like I'm just switching teams. you go down one rabbit hole and see how they are all connected. And I'm part of it [the problem]. I'm perpetuating it. I'm embarrassed by how much I listened to people who abused me in the past."*

IV

ONCE SARAH EMBRACED a new political reality, she scrubbed away one layer of confusion at a time. She began to see her mother's experience with Reagan and PATCO as a harbinger of things to come rather than an isolated event. Women were told that they could be just like men, and they found that to be partially true. The empty promise of salary and careerism revealed a naked truth: no one cares about you. There is no comfort, no security, no true safety in the fatal embrace of corporate servitude.

Women can elect to put their jobs before family, but they will always be second to profits for the companies who employ them. This has been men's reality since the first paycheck, but now women have equal access to the same bitter pill of uncertainty and powerlessness. If traditional life was tossed aside in the name of increasing women's independence, one day realizing you swapped out a caretaker husband and loving family for a heartless corporation must trigger a debilitating dissonance. As it turns out, corporate careers and faux financial security come with no-fault divorce clauses, just like modern marriages.

Sarah reexamined her entire life after the election.

"At this point, I'm so miserable, so unhappy, I'm willing to listen to anyone who is happy. I'm done pretending I know everything. I don't. The people I idolized, the people I thought were the good guys, were not the good guys. They were the assholes."

She reached out online to explore being a "red woman."

"The first thing I find out is that Republicans aren't bad people. Mind blown. They want the same things for their kids that I want for mine. And they seem so...

happy. Not like that manic, faked, forced kind, but genuinely happy. I asked them [Republican women], what is it about your life that makes you happy? And they all had the same answer: for the most part, things tend to work better when someone leads and someone follows. When you have someone who is looking out for you, looking after you, things are just better."

Communing with Trump supporters online introduced Sarah to a world of traditional women who loved their men and family more than their jobs. They found fulfillment and empowerment in a relationship where the man wasn't expected to be an equal in every way, but rather a comfortable complement with different and valuable attributes. Some even appreciated a husband who offered the relationship thoughtful leadership instead of mechanical deference.

This perspective clanged off Sarah's feminist programming like a wrench inside a dryer. She'd always demanded her husband be her equal, but such equality came with his acquiescence which, at the end of the day, she found unappealing. Her marriage had fallen into the banality and resentment that is common to many unions, and she wanted it to change. Sarah told me she had previously tried to control her husband and he let her. She set the agenda for the relationship and he went along with it. Neither one of them was happy and before discovering a different way online, they didn't know what to do. They feared they may be incompatible.

So Sarah tried a new approach: her husband would be number 1 and she would be 1A. She became the First Mate to his Captain and in doing so, reinvigorated her marriage with a traditional mindset that saw marriage as a union of complementary parts rather than a competition between equals. She relinquished control over her husband and the relationship, and he stepped up and became a leader. She focused more on taking care of the family at home, and he focused on their long-term security. To her pleasant surprise, this new strategy brought more satisfaction than her old ways. Sarah felt safer, more in love, and more appreciated than ever. For the first time in a long time, Sarah was content.

"I was promised I was going to be happy if I went to school, got good grades, and got a good job. Then I'd be happy. But that's a lie. A huge feminist lie."

DIMITRI

IMITRI'S FATHER TOLD him he was going to paradise. 17 days earlier he crammed his entire family and all their possessions on an ocean liner and headed for New York City. They left behind the family olive farm, leasing it to strangers for the first time in four generations. The time had come to leave the small village they called home. 23 kilometers south of Sparta, this was deep rural Greece. Their farm had sustained them for decades, but their future was in the U.S. Dimitri went from tending olive trees in Greece to dreaming of money trees in America. Hope for a brighter future warmed them as they crossed the ocean. Upon arrival in New York, their new life would begin.

When they arrived in 1968, the United States was on fire. Riots following the assassination of Martin Luther King, Jr. unleashed an angry darkness. Mobs smashed windows. Thieves looted inventory. Arsonists burned cities. US military units patrolled the neighborhoods of America's cities with unsheathed bayonets exposed and ready for action. The US Army and Reserves occupied parts of Washington, DC to restore peace and order. For America, waking up to a murdered King and a burning country, this was a living nightmare. The land of freedom and opportunity choked on racial divides and conflicted futures.

Dimitri hated his father for taking him to America. Nothing was like he promised. Instead of paradise, they found a country tearing itself apart. Instead of money trees, they found minimum wage. And instead of a warm welcome, Dimitri got a new name he didn't want. In the immigration lines of New York, the agent decided he was now James. Dimitri left his farm, his home, and even his identity back in Greece.

Questions of race and identity hit Dimitri as soon as he landed. American immigration paperwork required his family to state their racial identity, but there were only two options: white or black. Dimitri and his family never considered themselves to be white before. They were Mediterranean; they were Greek. But now they were white. They merely checked a box on paper. He didn't know this meant taking sides in a deep struggle.

> *"Every day I was picked on. I was bullied. I was getting thrown out every day. I got jumped every day by blacks. Because that was the thing, it was black vs. white. The Spanish [sic] community wasn't here yet. When they asked you your race back then it was white or black. I didn't even know what to call myself, so I check white. I'm Greek, not white. I have no connection to anyone living in England, but now, we're all white. I mean, I never thought of myself as white before I came [to America]."*

Eventually, they moved to Baltimore and got to work. His mother was a seamstress. His father cleaned churches and offices after-hours and Dimitri often tagged along, watching his old man pick up other people's trash and clean up their messes. Dimitri's first job was washing glasses at a restaurant for $5 a day. Sunny days on the farm in Greece seemed far away as he traded working the family land for working in someone else's kitchen. But his father kept reminding him, just work hard, make your way, and things will get better.

At age 19, Dimitri opened his first restaurant. It was a pizza joint in suburban Maryland. Slinging slices and sodas, each morsel of success drove him onwards. When his business became successful, he was able to sell the pizza place and flip it into an import business. After his father's death, Dimitri took over the family farm and began using it to produce high-quality olive oil, which he then imported to the United States. His business has grown so much he now imports not only from his father's estate but from that entire region in Greece. With multiple retail locations in the US and a thriving wholesale business, there's a chance you've tasted his olive oil if you live in the DC/Baltimore area. Evolving from migrant dishwasher to international businessman, decades later Dimitri finally realized his version of the American Dream.

Dimitri voted for Obama in 2008 and 2012. Everyone in his family is a Democrat. He was raised a Democrat. His wife and even his kids are Democrats. They were shocked to learn who Dimitri voted for in 2016. "My sons can't believe I voted for Trump. They know my history and they can't believe it." Until 2016, there was never a thought to vote Republican. But Trump came along and changed all of that for Dimitri, just as he did for nine million other Democrat to Deplorable voters.

"I voted with my feelings and my visions," he explained over lunch in DC. Dimitri took me to a restaurant which used his olive oil exclusively. "You let your instinct work; you have to. We're not going to any psychiatrist for help; you just let your instinct and feelings decide."

"I look at their face. I feel my feelings. What else can you get from a politician? They go in broke and come out rich. It's not like they're telling you the truth."

Dimitri didn't trust politicians. Maybe there was once a time where we believed politicians or the media, but a significant deficit developed as trust dissipated over the American landscape. Wikileaks revealed collusion between the Democratic National Committee and the major media outlets. Obama's promises to end the wars, close Guantanamo, and inflate the national psyche with hope fell flat. Hillary Clinton's tainted money trail, missing emails, and general duplicity shrouded her campaign. Simply put, the trust was gone.

When we can't use trust to make our decisions, we turn to feelings and emotions. Author and cartoonist Scott Adams believes persuasion made Trump's campaign successful. Based on Adam's past training as a hypnotist, he asserts Trump is a master persuader, someone who has a once in a generation ability to use words, imagery, and framing to evoke the desired emotional response. Trump wanted you to feel like he was with you, or that he was a man who understood you, the real you. From the Make America Great Again slogan, to catchphrases like "the Wall" and "lock her up," Trump used rhetoric to cut through the cacophony and reach people on an instinctual level. He energized people with his words. That resonated with people like Dimitri. Here is an immigrant, a one-time foreigner, the white not-white minority without a college education but an international business. What did Trump make him feel?

Dimitri explains,

"I love reality. I love real issues. I felt nothing for Hillary. She could never feel me. Trump said what he

said, and everyone tried to nitpick, you can't nitpick. He did say stupid stuff, but to me it was funny. Who cares?"

Dimitri mentioned to me three or four times that Trump spoke to his gut, that he felt Trump on a deeper level beyond policies or personalities. When people say something spoke to their gut what they mean is you're speaking to their instincts. Our instincts complement our rational thoughts to provide answers to tough questions. You can actually feel them in your body if you listen close enough.

The brain has two ways of communicating to us. On one hand, there is our inner monologue, which resides in the neocortex region of our brain, the land of rational thought and conscious decision making. This feature sets us apart from other animals and it evolved much later than the rest of our mind. On the other hand, the older more instinctual method of communication comes from our limbic system. This part of the brain observes the world around you and communicates with your body through visceral feelings in your gut or chest. These instincts developed long before our inner monologue was able to tell us what to do. So when people "go with their gut" or trust their "heartfelt emotions" they're not just talking crazy. In fact, they are relying on a sophisticated system which can process large amounts of data to answer complicated questions through signals like sweaty palms, increased heart-rates, and squirmy stomachs. People often go with their instincts because it just "feels" right. And in Election 2016, Trump used persuasion to push right past the new brain and speak directly to our old hearts.

Why would people be open to such persuasion? What was it about them or their situations which made emotional appeals to core instincts resonate enough to change life-long political affiliations? These are complex issues, but one reason is that Americans today are increasingly disconnected from the real world and may only sense it on a gut level.

Leftist narratives divorce us from reality. A fundamental assumption in postmodern philosophy, which influences the left, is an outright rejection of objective reality. Democrats often discard science and common sense. It's obvious when you consider the contradictions they put forth. Gender is a social construct yet transgenders can be born the wrong one. Diversity is the highest ideal, but a diversity of outcomes is unacceptable, and a diversity of opinions is intolerable. Equality for men and women is essential, but not when it comes to dangerous jobs, suicide rates, or family court. These among many other examples work together to alienate people from reality by pushing false assumptions about the natural world.

Political correctness also disconnects humans from reality. Language controls the mind as much as the mind controls language and to police our words is to pull levers in our brain. PC culture is a mind control tool of the left and people are weary. With Trump we had a candidate who threw off the handcuffs of political correctness and in doing so became the leader voters craved. By saying the wrong words, by being crass, by being angry and uncontrolled, Trump gave ordinary people in America hope, hope we could return to reality, back to a time when science and common sense ruled. In short, Trump offered a path upon which we could begin the slow dig back to enlightenment ideals rather than continue the tumble towards the blackness of postmodern and progressive anti-reality.

89% of Democrat to Deplorable voters agree or strongly agree with, "Fighting back against political correctness motivated me to vote in 2016."

Only 5% disagreed. The struggle to regain control over language as a path back to reality matters more to these voters than just about any other issue. My survey over-flowed with comments on PC culture:

"Political correctness is evil incarnate, and a desire to see it put down was highly motivating to me."

– White Male, Baby Boomer from Nevada City, CA.

"This was huge. I live in the SF area so everything is so offensive to everyone and I'm tired of it. It gets to the point where you are afraid to even express an opinion because it will be called hate speech or insensitive."

- White Female, Baby Boomer from Contra Costa, CA.

"Humans evolved to discriminate - to gather data and to use it to make the next judgment call. Somehow, after thousands and thousands of years, this has been deemed hateful. I do not understand."

- White Female, Millennial from Charleston, SC.

"I see a fixation with political correctness and speech policing as symptoms of a people in denial.

*Electing Trump would move the boundaries
of the conversation to force us to face the real-
life imperatives we've been protected from
by PC culture, and so save a lot of our lives.
Going "un-PC" certainly saved mine."*

- Black Male, Millennial from Richmond, RI.

Across the board, Democrat to Deplorable voters elected Donald Trump as a way to combat PC culture which encroaches on the First Amendment and manipulates our speech.

To live in a world where speech and thoughts are controlled is to live in a world divorced from reality. That world is chaotic. As humans, we fear the disordered; it is the wilderness, it is the darkness. Order and reason are the lights, and Trump led his voters back from the precipice of the underworld and returned them to reality. Though most voters lack the tools or education to describe this sensation, to me, it is self-evident from the data and stories I've heard over the last year.

It's not always easy to see the philosophies which produce daily politics and current events. Positions and policies often appear to swim in their own streams unattached to first principles. But they all build on their underlying ideologies. Clinton aligned herself with the progressive left, whose ideology of postmodernism rejects objective reality. Any idea which flows from that originating position can only lead to reality dislocations. If the foundation is a lie, then only lies may be built on top of it. Most normal people don't have time to read up on postmodernism, busy as they are with work and putting food on the table, but they certainly feel its ramifications. Because Clinton aligned with the postmodern left, she became the "chaos candidate," not Trump.

"I'm no longer a Democrat. If I cheat on my wife, that's it. I'm done. And I cheated on them. I'm done with being a Democrat." For Dimitri, he's done with the Democrats forever.

I

THE RUSH TO label all Trump voters as *white working class* erases people like Dimitri. While it is true his academic education ended with high school, it's also true he runs an international business. His work grows from a pristine Greek farm just outside of Sparta, all the way to retail outlets and farmer's markets across the Mid-Atlantic. He employs people on two continents and moves products and capital across oceans. Is this the portrait of an ignorant rural bumpkin? If you believe the media, all Trump voters are mouth-breathers who can barely sign their name. Dismissing the existence of people like Dimitri is part of the propaganda war waged by the left.

The lack of space for someone like Dimitri in the analysis of Trump supporters reveals the media's bias. Their blind spot could be the source of a future "surprise Democratic loss" in 2020, as they continue to ignore Dimitri and people like him. Waiving off all Trump supporters by calling them "white working class" is nothing more than the unrestrained snobbery of the pundit class.

According to my survey,

87% of Democrat to Deplorable voters finished at least some college, with 65% having undergraduate or graduate degrees.

These are not what you'd call uneducated people.

We know Democrat to Deplorable voters changed their minds after careful consideration. Educated people making the choice to ditch the Democrats in favor of Trump must mean something, so the media and Trump's haters have to diminish it. The media says there can't be thoughtful Trump supporters because that crashes the narrative. They forget about worldly "non-college" "whites" like Dimitri and ignore the credentialed Democrat to Deplorable voter on purpose. Pundits seem to be more interested in putting their head in the sand rather than admitting reality: not all Trump voters are rubes taken by a conman.

And let's not forget, Dimitri is also an immigrant. How is it that he could support Donald Trump and his alleged-ly xenophobic policies? Most Democrat's heads would ex-plode if they witnessed my lunch with Dimitri. Here he was, a brown-skinned immigrant with no college degree. He still spoke with an accent. And he spent a good while explaining to me how Trump was going to protect him from illegal immigration. This sort of thing just isn't possi-ble to the leftist media. To them, Trump was an unfettered xenophobe who'd unleash Hitler's hell on the country the day after inauguration. But to Dimitri, Trump was looking out for him.

"My whole family came here legally. We did the whole process. It took time, it cost a lot of money, but we did it the right way. Why can't everyone do it the right way?"

I've talked with many immigrants who came to the US through the system who feel the same. Somehow they're able to hear the distinction between illegal and legal immi-grant when Trump speaks. For them, their first American act was to respect and honor our immigration policies, while those who flaunt our laws and enter illegally are tainted with an original sin. To Dimitri, protecting the borders and ending illegal immigration was a celebration of his history, an acknowledgment that doing something the right way still had merit, that hard work, patience, and a little luck still formed the core of an American identity. To steal your place in our society was to poke Uncle Sam in the eye with a stick as you ran past him to grab your prizes.

When the Democrats and the left defend those who openly flaunt our laws, when they conspire to protect illegal aliens through sanctuary cities, when they devalue the time, toil, and devotion it takes to become a citizen the right way, they tell Dimitri and people like him: we just don't care about you.

> *"I'll vote for Trump again, of course, there is no reason not to. If the ocean is smooth, I'll vote for him. There is nothing the Democrats could ever do to get me back. I know too much now. They don't look big enough; they don't see far enough. That's how I feel."*

GEORGE

"I hated how he first came out against immigrants, because my whole family is immigrants. I'm not gonna lie, I hated what he said about Mexicans."

THE DRIVE FROM Washington DC to York, Pennsylvania takes a couple of hours. The dense city morphs into suburban office parks and eventually fades into tree covered rolling hills. In time, the farms start and you get the sense you've gone from one America to another. Instead of people from all over the world mashed on top of each other, you can relax and breath and expand into the rural countryside. The pressure of city life releases with each mile heading north. Rainbow flags and BLM yard signs recede, and in their place come gun shops and Cracker Barrels, colonial era historic sites, and signs for ammunition. This America and Washington, DC feel like distant cousins. They may have met once at a funeral or wedding but they share no life together beyond a great grandmother somewhere.

I chose York County, PA because it is the capital of Red State Pennsylvania. It's not a Philadelphia suburb, or Pittsburgh where voting blue is expected. York represents the "other" part of PA that gets little attention. PA is now red and York is one of the main reasons. Trump beat Hillary in Pennsylvania overall by a mere 44,000 votes.[31] But in York County he dominated her by 60,000, while in

2012 Romney beat Obama by only 40,000. Trump expanded the margin of victory by 50%. You can slice and dice the numbers a million ways, but without York, Trump would have a hard time winning this key state. It's safely Trumpland now. Despite being solidly red, there is a tight immigrant population in York which has always voted Democrat and that's who I was interested in.

I reached out to my people on Twitter and connected with a man whose family owns a busy diner just outside of York City. "The Astoria Diner" on West Market Street is a local favorite, hopping like a scene from movie. Waitresses in pink dresses, dropped ceiling tiles, vinyl covered tablecloths. The coffee cups are small, but the refills are endless. In another era, the air would have been thick with cigarette smoke as the grill churned out hash browns and fried eggs. It was the kind of place where $15 dollars could buy you half the menu. A few red MAGA hats mixed in with green John Deere baseball caps. Service with a smile, "would you like some more coffee, Hun?"

I sat down with George Margetas, a one-time Democrat who now serves the on the local GOP Committee. His whole family are still Democrats, but they, like him, voted for Trump. "Well, everyone except Mom," he says. Though his mother never came around, George was on board from the start.

George explained over coffee:

"I was behind Trump from the very beginning, someone different from the normal establishment candidates. Jeb Bush, Rubio, the same group of guys. It didn't matter to me, Republican or Democrat, I just needed something outside of the establishment,"

This wasn't a new feeling for him, however. This readiness for change had been developing for many years.

> *"I didn't like George Bush either, he lied to me.*
> *Bill Clinton was the best President we ever had."*

Democrat to Deplorable voters often cite a general dissatisfaction with the establishment as large as a reason they voted for Trump. To them the "establishment" isn't limited to just one party.

According to my survey, 85% of Democrat to Deplorable voters consider both parties to be the "establishment."

> *"I understood the hope and change of Obama, but when it comes to him and George Bush, they were the worst. The Trump thing was a rejection of both Obama and George W. Bush. Around here, people were still pissed off about being lied to. I didn't like being lied to by George Bush. I didn't think going to Iraq was the right move."*

The Iraq war came up in several of my interviews. Sure, Bush lead us into that war, but everyone remembers that Hillary voted, "yes." To us, Hillary, Obama, Bush, Bill Clinton- they were the establishment and we were over it.

Still, despite the groundswell of anti-establishment feelings, supporting Trump wasn't always the easiest, especially for a family of immigrants.

"I hated how he first came out against immigrants, because my whole family is immigrants. I'm not gonna lie, I hated what he said about Mexicans."

George referred to Trump's opening comments of the campaign where he mentioned Mexican immigrants and rapists: "When Mexico sends its people, they're not sending their best. They're not sending you. They're not sending you. They're sending people that have lots of problems, and they're bringing those problems with us. They're bringing drugs. They're bringing crime. They're rapists. And some, I assume, are good people."[32]

George says he was able to look past this because he understands negotiating. As a criminal defense attorney he negotiates every day. Sometimes you have to start wide to find a middle, "I told a lot of my friends who were scared, relax. The only way to get what you think is a fair resolution is to go to the other edge where you seem unreasonable. Then you find a compromise in the middle."

The willingness to view Trump's comments, whatever they may be, in a favorable light is a common theme. In fact, the direct way Trump speaks, right to the gut, is something that drew people in from the beginning. In this day of political correctness, frank and offensive conversation is downright rebellious, and Democrat to Deplorables, George and his family included, were ready to rebel. Trump's speech patterns and style drew them in despite the words. It was the act of unrestricted speaking which carried weight, not even necessarily what was said.

> *"I grew up in PC culture. There's things I always wanted to say but I couldn't. He finally put a voice to it."*

I

THE FRONTIER OF PC culture pushes forward every day as it converts the acceptable to the forbidden. The definition of offensive changes and each new level of outrage is more preposterous than the rest. In fall of 2015, three girls at the University of Wisconsin-Plattsville learned just how ridiculous things have gotten. Other students reported them to the authorities for their Halloween costume: sunglasses which were meant to identify them as the Three Blind Mice.[33] The girls were forced to remove the costumes and take down pictures from social media because they were deemed offensive to blind people.

Halloween is increasingly tense on other college campuses as well. In late 2015, a Yale lecturer asked, "Is there no room anymore for a child or young person to be a little bit obnoxious, a little bit inappropriate or provocative or, yes, offensive?" Students exploded with outrage at these seemingly reasonable remarks. Apparently, they were offended at the idea of being offended. One could dismiss this incident as just college kids being stupid, but the backlash forced the teacher to resign.[34] The country appears to be moving away from a culture which demands and rewards free speech towards one where you better watch what you say and do out of fear of being reported.

College campuses have created bias response teams (BRT) to crackdown on offensive thoughts, words and behaviors. If kids see or hear something they don't like, now they have an official mechanism by which to report their peers. It's kind of like a kid-run thought police whose purpose is to protect people from things that hurt their feelings. People have to watch what they think and do at all times now or else the bias response team will come a-knocking. The Foundation for Individual Rights in Education (FIRE) reports there were 218 BRT's on campuses in 2016.

From their report in 2017:

"Bias Response Teams, when armed with open-ended definitions of "bias," staffed by law enforcement and student conduct administrators, and left without training on freedom of expression, represent an emerging risk to free and open discourse on campus and in the classroom. Bias Response Teams create — indeed, they are intended to create — a chilling effect on campus expression."

It's easy to see how Trump appealed to those who felt controlled. People who were tired of being lied to by politicians, people who were fed up with having to avoid certain words in certain places, people who felt like their individual liberty was at risk - these people heard Trump on a different level than Democrats and the media. George explained, "He spoke to them in a language they could understand. Even if they didn't like what they heard, they were glad someone said it."

At the same time Trump was reaching people on gut level, Hillary was on the campaign trail doing the opposite. After she made her infamous "deplorable" speech, it was clear even to these long-time Democrats, the time for change was now.

"The deplorable speech hurt her so much. Professional people. Working class people. Mothers and daughters. Any of you who voted for Trump are losers. She went into the gutter and lost any credibility she had. She hurt herself so much with that. The local residents here got all that info from Facebook - it spread quickly via text, private message. She didn't have the charisma to recover from that."

Trump spoke and the people of York PA listened. Hillary opened her mouth and stuck her foot in it.

The Clinton campaign thought Pennsylvania would always be blue. They thought it was part of an impenetrable blue wall which assured her victory. But the noxious atmosphere from DC spread up Interstate 70 and smothered the people of the Keystone State. The fumes were toxic enough to convert even lifelong Democrats to Trump supporters. George's family had been Democrats in a Republican part of the state, daring to be blue in a cloud of red. But Hillary was just too nasty.

For the George and the people of York, preventing a Hillary presidency was just as important as supporting Trump. Many Obama-Trump voters felt the same way.

According to my survey, 84% of Democrat to Deplorable voters agreed or strongly agreed with the following statement, "Being anti-Hillary Clinton motivated me to vote in 2016."

For Democrat to Deplorable voters the election in 2016 was about self-preservation. Hillary made it that way. There was no hemming or hawing when it came time to vote. The Deplorables loved their candidate and hated the opposition.

The people of York, Pennsylvania turned out in huge numbers because they knew Hillary despised them, too. She thought they were all irredeemable Deplorables and she let everyone know. Who knew how a Hillary Clinton Presidency would have treated those she and her supporters thought were beyond the pale. Republicans and former Democrats who supported Trump weren't willing to take their chances on Clinton's mercy. If she hated them now while she still needed their vote, what would she do when she had the most powerful job in the world?

LISA

LISA'S MOTHER WORKED the grill at the only restaurant in town. Their small mining village had one hotel and a convenience store, which served all 200 people who lived there. Her family moved to eastern Oregon so her father could work at the mining company, but in time, the company left town and her father left the family. It was just Lisa, her three brothers, and a hardworking single mom who dealt with hot grease and brusque orders all day. There was no shame in their poverty, to Lisa it was just life. Eastern Oregon is dotted with ghost towns of mining cities gone bust, and her hometown was on its way there. If it wasn't for the ranching industry surrounding the valley, Lisa's town would have died.

It would have been easy for Lisa to stay in her hometown living a simple yet grinding life many would consider to be "white working class." While Mom didn't have a college degree, and neither did Dad, Lisa was determined to live a life bigger than the one offered at home. One day at school she found a flyer for a summer program at Stanford University. 17 year old Lisa was excited to see California and discover new things, but it was too expensive. Even with a scholarship she was still $3,000 short. The tantalizing prospect of a new future teased her as the weight of her mother's poverty held her down.

But Lisa's spirit was bigger than just a few thousand dollars. She wasn't going to let money ruin her dream to see the world and grow beyond a dying industrial town in the backwaters of the United States. So she took control. She wrote a letter to the nearby ranchers, asking them for help. In return for a small donation, Lisa explained how she would become a lawyer and promised to take on the "globalist meat industry" to save the local ranchers from Argentine steaks eroding the last remaining way of life in her town. After a rancher made a donation of $20 or $50, they passed her letter on. Her small town rallied behind her and donated the entire $3,000. Lisa's new life was about to start.

Lisa's summer experience at Stanford changed her in ways she hadn't expected as the University and its students revealed a way of life she'd never experienced. She expected to learn about politics and law for the first time. She knew she was going to learn how to give a speech and debate big ideas. But what she didn't anticipate was the culture shock. Lisa met an Asian person for the first time on Stanford's campus. In the hallways and between classes she overheard students talking about violin lessons and SAT prep classes. Kids mentioned international trips and extended vacations provided by Mom and Dad. Lisa had leapt from a dying mining town to an international hotspot. The jarring contrast changed her perspective. Her brief time at Stanford threw open the doors of the world and all she wanted was to run right through them. Imagine being the poor girl from rural Oregon surrounded by 1%'er children at Stanford. It was like she wore ratty jeans to a black-tie gala. It was Lisa's first real experience with the global elite and she wanted to join them.

The next several years for Lisa wouldn't be as exciting as that summer at Stanford. Though she applied there for undergrad, she didn't get in. So she settled for a university in Idaho, earning dual degrees in economics and history.

Even there, money remained a constant issue. Each summer she returned to Oregon to clean hotel rooms and hustle up a school years' worth of expenses. After she graduated, Lisa stayed at the university to teach. Life was 'ok,' but the memory of Stanford lingered. Within a couple of years, she was ready to make the big jump. She moved to New York City and attended Columbia Law School with a focus on human rights and social justice. Afterwards, Lisa landed a job in international development. Her path from country bumpkin to big city career woman was complete.

Lisa was always an advocate. Whether it was working after school to help her mother, fighting for the local ranchers, or looking out for the impoverished world-wide - Lisa just wanted to help despite her modest beginnings. Whether it was poverty, a lack of opportunity, or challenges of class mobility, Lisa overcame them all. She was now an international development specialist working to solve global problems like poverty, housing, and education for the poorest of the poor. She whisked around the world helping people in need. Myanmar, Kuwait, China, South Africa, East Europe. Lisa saw and touched places she'd only visited in books. And now at 34, she was a single white female in Brooklyn, living the life. Lisa had arrived.

Lisa voted for Barack Obama in both 2008 and 2012. She "thought Barack Obama was the best America had to offer. With him, we could be a multicultural democracy. We could be a smart technocracy." Lisa too was inspired by Obama's messages of hope and change. She admired the man and believed he could inspire us all to be better citizens at home and around the world. Lisa's support for Obama was a source of pride. She never once considered the alternatives in '08 or '12. It was Obama all the way for her and for everyone she knew. The lighting in her life was all blue. When it came time for the 2016 election, one would have thought Hillary Clinton was a no brainer; a vote for "her" seemed like the only option. Add in the opportunity to elect the first woman President and it seemed like a slam dunk.

But something wasn't sitting right with Lisa. After 2012, her perspective began to shift. Her work in global development began to make her feel uneasy. She started to question what she was doing and what she believed. As she moved capital and ideas around the world trying to lift people up, her own psyche was deflating. She became disconnected from her work. Joining the ranks of the global elite didn't fill Lisa with pride and satisfaction, nor did it allow her to help the people she really cared about. Instead her experiences tore off globalism's shiny veneer and exposed to her a dark underbelly filled with hypocrisy, poor decision making, and negative outcomes.

I

INTERNATIONAL DEVELOPMENT IS essential to the globalist structure. International banks facilitate massive infrastructure projects, which are funded by equally massive debt. Institutions like the InterAmerican Development Bank, the World Bank, and private firms help developing countries by facilitating access to capital. The development financed by this debt is meant to bring improved infrastructure like new roads, power plants, and utility services, or new investment in local industries like mining, oil, or gas. The goal is that engagement with the first world will bring institutional development, advances in democracy, and increased standards of living to countries wallowing at the bottom of the world order.

But to gain access to this money, poor countries have to adopt certain neoliberal policy prescriptions. While these practices are said to be in the developing country's best interest, they also have the effect of wrapping third world countries into the globalist system. Creditors demand the country be opened to the globalized network with few obstacles. Goods, services, money and investment must be free to move in and out of the country with low or no taxes. The countries' budgets must prioritize paying interest on the debt, subordinating domestic services to the demands of bankers in New York, London, and Washington, D.C.

Low trade barriers, free capital flows, budget austerity, and a floating exchange rate - ideas once known as the Washington Consensus - are required of the third world by the first. And as it turns out, the net result isn't always to help the world's needy, but to fatten the global elite through a feast on poor people. From South America, to Eastern Europe, and across Africa, countries which rely heavily on external financing for development often find their autonomy limited and their people suffering.

Once Lisa began to see how this system really worked, she became concerned. Projects continuously failed to meet the high ideals she brought out of school. Over time Lisa became painfully aware of the tangible damage her work was inflicting. One project in particular stood out.

A Canadian company wanted to expand a mining operation in Latin America. It was Lisa's job to assess the project's impact on the region's local population. Her research showed that an additional mine would make a bad situation even worse. She believed the mine would poison the local drinking water, strip people of land rights, displace them from their homes, and burden the country with millions of dollars of debt. It was a terrible deal for the local population, but a great one for the mining company.

"Essentially they [the mining company] were stealing the gold, giving the local people nothing while the mine makes millions and millions of dollars per year. Their water was poisoned. Their culture was destroyed. They've been pushed off their land onto a tiny little sliver so small they couldn't even grow food anymore. And they had no control over their community or culture. Their laws were even being dictated by a foreign corporation."

She presented these findings to her bosses, arguing that the project ran contrary to the organization's goals, that the people and the environment of the country would be damaged far more than they would be helped, and there was no way she could support the expansion. But despite Lisa's onclusions, the project went ahead as planned. So instead of working to help poor people improve their standing, Lisa now found herself assisting in their demise. None of development's warm and fuzzy goals were being met here. The local people weren't benefiting, no institutions were being developed, no sense of democracy was being enhanced. Only the financiers and the mining company were winning as they destroyed poor people and the environment in the process. The extraction of precious resources at the expense of helpless indigenous people wasn't why Lisa went to school. She was disgusted.

"I wanted to use the global system to lift people out of poverty, not make things worse."

Ultimately, Lisa's work had brought her face to face with the perils of international development. The work she idealized as a student turned out to damage, not help, the people she cared about. After this case and a few more like it she was fed up with the whole thing.

> "The entire idea of development is useless. Some countries have improved, the ones which did had some kind of governance and drive from within to develop. The ones who didn't, were exploited. Development from the outside doesn't work, all that happens is the elite of those countries become enriched."

II

By 2016, Lisa evolved from an eager true believer to a discouraged cynic. The industry she idealized took her unbound optimism and ground it into a growing skepticism. She'd lost trust in the system she once believed in after the system revealed itself to be full of lies and contradictions. As Election 2016 began to heat up and Lisa was bombarded with messages from all sides, she turned her skeptical eye towards American politics. Lots of people were telling her lots of stories, but were any of them true?

In Lisa's New York social and professional circles, Nationalism is a dirty word and nationalists are horrible people. To the liberal elite Lisa ran with, nationalism is a xenophobic hate-filled ideology associated with Hitler and the Nazis. Globalism, on the other hand, is humane, kind, and honorable. These two positions are so ingrained that to question one or the other is suicide. If one wants to work in international development, they must repeat "globalism good" and "nationalism bad" over and over like a mantra.

But Lisa had seen dark side of development. She'd seen through the lies of globalism first hand and understood how she was manipulated by teachers, the media, and global institutions. Her growing skepticism nudged to her examine other ideas she'd always assumed were true. Questions she would have never considered began to bubble up into her consciousness. Lisa was fooled by globalism, maybe she was wrong about nationalism too?

Her work in international development revealed a sad truth: globalists do not care much for democracy. To Lisa, "democracy is about making meaningful decisions about your country." When she saw how the international system worked to disenfranchise poor people in third world countries for the benefit of financiers and international corporations, she saw how the global elite didn't care about democracy and self-governance. In fact, political disenfranchisement of the working class only worked to fatten the rich even further.

"There is an open conspiracy of international elites who want to erode nation states through continued neoliberal policies and poorly enforced immigration laws, which will lead to the formation of a sort of world government, and to me, there is no way that can be democratic."

Part of the neoliberal agenda is to reduce barriers to immigration and it generally has bipartisan support. Both parties want new immigrants to the U.S. for cheap labor, and the Democrats get the added advantage of extra votes. Neither party is doing it for humanitarian reasons.

"The thing about neoliberalism in general is that it's all about wages. That's the crazy thing about immigration. You're a moral monster if you're against open borders, but really, what's happening is that there is a separate legal system. Essentially the United

States is an apartheid. We have one system for legal residents and another quasi-legal system for illegal immigrants. These are people who are desperately poor, and we encourage and abet them in coming here so we can take advantage of them for their wage resources."

The United States sends clear signals to poor people around the world that our doors are open. We promise to protect them from immigration authorities if they settle in one of our many sanctuary cities.[35] We offer them welfare and travel assistance if they are underage and traveling alone. Major jurisdictions like Washington, DC, San Francisco, Chicago, Philadelphia and New York City publicly announce that even if an illegal immigrant commits a crime, they will be shielded from federal agents. And along the way they consume public services paid for by legal American residents. When federal laws are ignored and resources are devoted to supporting illegal aliens, democracy is eroded in the process. Why have laws and policies if they aren't enforced? Money, that's why. The elite in the United States want wage competition among the poor in order to make the fat cats fatter. And if you oppose them, you're branded as a bigot or a racist.

"I'm totally on board with Nationalism. Nationalists aren't motivated by xenophobia, racism, or Islamophobia. It's about self-determination and protecting the rights of citizens."

Her work in international development clued Lisa in to the way globalism eroded personal autonomy and civil rights abroad. She saw how global elites conspired to destroy other cultures for the sake of a dollar, and now she could see the same destruction at home. So when Donald

Trump started talking about the international cabal she knew intimately, she knew he was right. Trump's words resonated with her experience. Lisa had finally kicked her brainwashing and was ready to listen.

Other Democrat to Deplorable voters felt the same way:

"Globalist policies will weaken a country and its culture. Nationalist policies will strengthen a country's culture allowing individuals achieve their potential."

- White Male, Boomer from Shaker Heights, OH.

"Globalism enriches only the very rich, and marginally, and unevenly helps the very poor. Nationalism helps those within a nation."

- Mixed-race Male, Generation X from Denver, CO.

"Globalism rewards countries that diminish its citizens quality of life in order to maximize profits. Nationalism is a concept that empowers its nation's citizens to work hard for one another to ensure the nation thrives."

- White Male, Generation X from Port St. Lucie, FL.

According to my survey, 90% of Democrat to Deplorable voters agree with the following statement, "The trend toward a global economy is a bad thing for our country."

Trump's anti-globalist and pro-nationalist rhetoric severed the last remaining thread connecting Lisa to the Democrats. Though she voted for Obama in both 2008 and 2012, Lisa had changed too much to toe the party line in election 2016. Hillary Clinton offered more of the same: free trade, open borders, and a disdain for people who wanted to put America first. Lisa knew first hand that Clinton's worldview was flawed and bad for America. Trump was the only one speaking to Lisa's experience, reflecting back to her an understanding of the world that made sense. Make America Great Again and "build the wall" hammered home for Lisa that Trump was the only choice. Lisa officially ditched the Democrats and embraced being a Deplorable. Despite being surrounded by progressive blue liberals in New York City, Lisa made the bold choice to come out to her friends as a Trump supporter. What happened next only reassured Lisa she'd made the right choice. There was no going back.

In January 2017, an 18 year old man with special needs was kidnapped and tortured for being a Trump supporter. Inexplicably, the kidnappers live-streamed themselves beating, abusing, and humiliating the man on Facebook. In the video you can hear them say, "Fuck Donald Trump. Fuck white people." The live-stream was only 30 minutes, but the man was held hostage for nearly four hours as he bled profusely from his multiple wounds.[36]

Lisa found the video on social media. Watching it made her chest and stomach tighten with disgust and fear. She watched four people beat and torture a man for his political views. The visceral fear and anxiety of seeing such violence committed over thoughts and ideas, ideas Lisa herself may have, began to smother any of her remaining hope. She worried her brothers back home might be next. Hell, even Lisa herself could be next.

Lisa hoped an outrageous hate crime like this would have spurred a national conversation. The mass media should have seized upon this violent act, denounced political violence and implored their viewers to discourage such behavior among their friends and family. But she was mistaken. There was no empathy. There was no national conversation explaining Trump voters were human who simply held differing political views. No, it appeared Trump supporters deserved what they had coming and if they got beat up for their politics, then so be it.

When Lisa later shared the video with her roommate, she expected her to sympathize and share in Lisa's shock and horror. Instead, the roommate laughed.

"Well, he is a Trump supporter," she said.

The callousness of her roommate's reaction wasn't due to the distance from the event or the sterilizing effect of video. To Lisa, it was a manifestation of brainwashing which reduced Trump supporters to something less than an animal, which meant Lisa was less than animal too. It was one thing to know there were unsympathetic monsters out there in the world, it was another to find yourself living with one. Lisa was sickened and afraid.

To these New York liberals, who've all dabbled with veganism or cruelty free shampoos, Trump supporters didn't register on their empathy radar. A Trump voter's value was somewhere below mindless factory chickens. The media, the liberal elites, and the Democrats all worked in unison to demote Trump supporters to sub-human. Sub-chicken even.

Lisa thought to herself, "I'm living in crazy land." All election season, the media bombarded Lisa's roommate with messages that Trump supporters were "monsters, literal genocidal maniacs who weren't human anymore" and they deserved cruelty. That rhetoric did its job, and empathy vanished across the country, especially in New York City.

She reached out to a colleague at work the following day, expecting, or maybe wishing, this next person would reassure her that the humanity hadn't completely died in her social circle.

She asked her friend about the video. His response, "It's not as bad because he's white."

New York social justice circles, lawyers, well-educated people discounted violence because the victim didn't share their love of Hillary Clinton. Our nation's elite, dismissed heinous acts because the victim was white. In their world, only minorities can be victims - the white male is always the perpetrator. The brainwashed liberals sound eerily similar to rape apologists who say the victim had it coming because of what she was wearing. These people excused violence against a white Trump supporter because of his skin color and the candidate he supported.

Lisa's friends abandoned her. One asked, "It's 1933, Lisa, where do you stand?" as they cast her aside as a Nazi. Despite her tireless work for social justice around the world and how she worked every day to help the less fortunate, Lisa's friends ostracized her because of her political views. She understood she wasn't welcomed any longer. Her journey from rural Oregon to the Big City was over. She made plans to leave international development and move closer to home. By 2018, Lisa left New York and her dream job behind in a cloud of sadness and confusion.

Imagine finding out everything you were you taught and advocated for was a lie. Imagine coming to understand the work you were doing wasn't helping the needy but enriching the greedy? Imagine the guilt, shame, and even horror of participating in the very system you thought you were subverting?

As her time wound down in New York, Lisa felt guilty for abandoning her roots. When the ranchers paid for Lisa to attend Stanford, they had no idea they were planting the seeds of a liberal globalist. But that's what she became. And in time it horrified her. The contradiction between where she came from and what she became was an apt metaphor for America in 2016.

Donald Trump's campaign didn't so much cause the rift between nationalist and globalists, as it tore the shroud away and revealed the new civil war waging in America. As Lisa suffered her mind-melting experience, so too was the country having its own trauma. Minds, perspectives, realities - all shattered across the board. Donald Trump focused the national conversation on the dirty little secret: America was at war with itself and the first casualties were coming home. Just like Lisa.

Section Three

The Big Finish

STAGNATION

WHEN NINE MILLION voters ditched the Democrats and switched to the Republicans, it was a big deal. The decision to abandon a lifelong affiliation to support an outsider who promised to blow things up doesn't happen without a reason. Nine million people who voted for Obama were ready for something different because despite the slogans and promises, Obama's hope and change delivered despair and stagnation. He presided over an era which ground down large swaths of the American people, where some of them became trapped in economic distress and even death spirals. Wars raged on, real economic growth withered, and a health epidemic swept the nation. Hard structural forces created the Trump moment, and Obama presided over eight years of their development.

What was Obama's legacy? How did the world look and feel as his second term wound down? What did he leave for the next president? Did Obama leave the country better than he found it?

To us Deplorable voters Obama left a stagnant mess of broken promises. He promised a hopeful future but instead dimmed the lights and left us searching around in the dark for answers. Surely some things were bigger than his sales pitch and beyond his control, but that's the point. Trump was born out of decades of stagnation with an Obama climax. So where should we start?

The wars in the Mideast continued their ascent into Orwellian constancy as troops remained in Afghanistan and elsewhere. Soldiers who weren't even born on 9/11/01 will soon be fighting in Asia. Millennials have no idea what a "peace dividend" is. Our armies fought behind the scenes and out of sight, unless it's your son. Obama promised to reign in our war machine and was unable. In fact, he expanded our drone assassination programs, sending flying robot killers into foreign countries to drop bombs on combatants and their families instead of bringing the troops home and inching us closer to peace.

The economy sputtered for the middle class despite top level growth in gross domestic product. Real wages were virtually the same as they were in the 1960s meaning the average American has the same earning power as 50 years ago.[37] Does that seem like progress? And while the middle class was no better off the previous generations, the wealthiest had more than ever. The richest 20% of the country controlled 84% of the wealth. While 40%, almost half of us, controlled only 0.4%.[38] Less than 1% of the wealth for nearly half the nation!

And Obama should get the blame. Despite acknowledging inequality to be the greatest challenge of the early 21st Century, he still presided over the most dramatic increase of income inequality in our lifetime.[39] After the 2008-2009 crisis, Obama's administration bailed out wall street with taxpayer money, letting the crooked bankers who devastated the country walk away scot-free with billions of dollars in their pockets and not a single moment of jail time. Obama's version of protecting the little guy resulted in higher incomes and wealth for the rich, and foreclosures and stagnation for the rest.

With such a disheartening economic outlook, some Americans turned to drugs. The opioid crisis in America can be thought of as a great escape from a depressing today and a bleaker tomorrow. Does this sound like hope and change? The epidemic is now worse than AIDS ever was and causes more deaths than even auto accidents. The white middle class, once the undeniable heartbeat of America now sputters and dies of sickness and neglect. Opioids kill people and the economy. But which came first? It hardly matters as the death spiral chews up some 40,000 lives and $150 billion in economic losses per year.[40] Mortality rates for white Americans now rise as they decline for minorities.[41] People are literally dying from Obama's version of hope and change.

If there was something to look forward to, perhaps people would have felt differently in 2016, but the outlook is bleak. Maybe there will be a fancy new technology which will lead to fresh boom times and a massive rising tide that lifts all boats. That's the way it's worked in the past with the industrial revolution, railroads, cars, planes, and the internet. But the new technologies on the way aren't saviors for the middle class, they're just more body blows. Driverless vehicles promise to kill truck drivers, one of the last jobs for non-college white men in middle America now that manufacturing has exited the country. Artificial intelligence isn't creating jobs for displaced truck drivers or coal miners either. In fact, depending on technology to bring another economic boom seems like a bad bet. While major technological revolutions can bring high growth and low unemployment, they also can bring disruption by erasing sectors of the economy.

But technology corporations still don't see anything big coming down the road. They continue to hoard trillions of dollars of cash rather than invest it. These companies, those closest to the technological evolution, those with the best eye for tomorrow, would rather get passbook interest than invest in our future, an unprecedented, remarkable, and even terrifying reality.[42] With a gun to their head and shareholders demanding profits, our industrial leaders think their best bet is a 1% government bond. If our tech and manufacturing giants don't want to invest in America and Americans, who will?

And to make things even worse, eight years after Obama's historic election, racial tensions seem as bad as they've ever been in my lifetime. The historic arc of reconciliation has halted and animus grows where love once sprouted. Author and social critic Ta-Nehisi Coates blames Trump voters for creating the national mood, but he's wrong. He lays the "bloody heirloom" of white supremacy at our feet.[43] But he fails to acknowledge how Trump won the election in an environment which had been building for decades but climaxed under Obama.

Obama delivered the nation unto Trump, and that is his legacy.

Nine million Democrats voted for Obama thinking they were part of solving our fathers' problems, but eight years of his leadership transformed us and the country in some twisted way which left us preferring the name Deplorable to Democrat. We gave Obama a chance and regretted it, and that regret manifested itself in a golden-haired orange-faced reality TV star. I can't imagine a sadder way for Obama to end his Presidency than to come face-to-face with his replacement, Donald Trump.

Behind every Democrat to Deplorable voter lurked a shapeless antagonist, a sort of cosmic horror with no name, felt everywhere and nowhere at the same time. It's hard to nail down just what ails you when your feelings are the result of decades worth of toxic ideas, government policies, and epic wars.

It is nearly impossible for voters to identify the forces of discontent that swirl around them and many settle for simple shorthand. Obama. The Left. Immigrants. Globalists. Trump voter's instincts tell them something is wrong. The forces which create this unease are vast and operating on a historic time scale rather than on a day-to-day schedule most people can process. Voters aren't equipped to assess the impact of globalization in their lives or understand how feminist ideology works to influence their relationships today. Who can blame them when they're busting their ass putting food on the table? Who has time to research the latest political happenings when jobs are hard to come by? Who has the energy to read up on the latest twists in philosophy when a drug epidemic ravages our country?

When people voted in 2016 they were searching for comfort. For some, what they wanted was just a chance to feel better. When they pulled the lever they wished they'd get a happy pill in return. For others, they sought revenge, and for them the voting booth was more executioner's chambers than a doctor's office. In either case it was massive, stormy, chaotic forces pushing them to make a change, and it wasn't Trump who created the negativity.

Obama failed to deliver on his promises. His election did bring a fleeting hope, but it fizzled under the heat of failure. Obama was my guy and I felt like he owed me. I gave him my vote and in exchange I wanted the soaring hope he promised. But beyond that, I wanted real solutions to real problems. I wanted the US to withdraw from

Afghanistan and the Middle East. I wanted Obama to solve the global financial crisis and punish those responsible. I wanted a humane solution to the foreclosure crisis. And I wanted greater unity among my fellow Americans.

When I voted for Obama, when the country elected him, it felt as though we moved into a post-racial world, where a black man could lead and unite us. Obama gave me hope that racial antagonism was in the past and the imminent future would be color blind. Maybe I thought an Obama vote came bow-tied in absolution for whatever white guilt I carried. Maybe I asked too much of Obama, as none of my hopes came to be.

Wars, drugs, death, stagnant wages, the shadow of incomprehensible inequality, and the resurgence in racial animosity. For our Democrat to Deplorable voters, as crazy as it seems, this is just the setting for the story, not the even the main plot. No, the despair and stagnation delivered by Obama is just the introduction. What follows is a summary of several lines of thinking, which when taken together will present the modern circumstances that lead to Obama's voters ditching the Democrats and giving us Donald Trump.

The review is broad and will jump around from economics to philosophy to the media and back, with my goal to memorialize the current zeitgeist in book form as reference for the lived experience of myself, my subjects, the survey respondents, and the nine million Obama to Trump voters who on that crazy day in November 2016 changed the election and perhaps the nation.

GLOBALISM IS ANTI-NATIONALIST HORROR

Globalism. This word can evoke starkly different feelings depending on what circle you run in. If you live in New York City and work in international development like Lisa did, globalism is a radiating ball of opportunity and excitement. Being a globalist is sexy. You get to travel and connect with alluring foreign cultures, escape the drudgery of everyday American life and immerse yourself in something exotic. New foods, new languages, new people. All so separate and distinct from "America" that somehow it's obviously just better.

College graduates from elite schools don't plan two months of rail travel across the industrial Midwest, instead they hop on the euro rail and track the well-worn ant trail of American travelers, following the breadcrumbs left by last year's senior class. It all feels adventurous and bold, despite being wholly unoriginal. But this manufactured sexiness isn't globalism per se, it's simply an international perspective, an orientation to outside things, rather than an appreciation for what is home.

Though returning from extended stays abroad often creates an appreciation for some things you left behind, the general fetishization of international travel by the college educated elite masks a darker reality. Globalism isn't just a taste for authentic Italian food or the search for the next great youth hostel, it's a purposefully destructive force whose predictable side effects are unemployment, alienation, disenfranchisement, and ultimately cultural death.

If you're a middle class American outside the big cities, with little or no college education, and no spare change or spare time to run through Germany on a beer garden tour, globalism has a very different meaning. Globalism is the faceless specter, an amorphous demon eviscerating your home and family without ever confronting you directly. You've lost a great and decisive battle without ever seeing your foe on the battlefield. Factories just close with the shades pulled down and a vacancy sign posted. The machines grind to a halt and then vanish in liquidation sales. The paychecks end, the work whistle falls silent, and with it your way of life evaporates.

Globalism is nowhere and everywhere. It is the cosmic horror which cannot be touched but which rips and tears at your flesh giving you no chance to fight back, no chance to defend yourself, and no moment of dignity. If you've lived your entire life in one town, globalist forces from the other side of the world invisibly descending on your home must feel like a malevolent god capriciously deciding today was the end. When competition for your job is on the other side of the globe, it may as well be a fiction. If you can't see them, can't touch them, and can't fight them, are they not god-like?

Globalization in reality is a collection of policies, perspectives, and inevitability. The world has grown up and the United States isn't the only place making the things we Americans want. Sometimes buying a TV from Asia makes more sense: it's cheaper and often better. The straightforward comparison of domestic material products to foreign made ones is a concrete and tangible representation of life in a globalized world. Various government policies and agreements opened trade between us and the rest of the world. The result was a nice cheap TV for the living room. But there's more to it than that. Neoliberal economic policies not only advocate for open trade, but for money and people to freely move from country to country as they see fit.

Neoliberal globalism is a three-legged stool. If you implement one without the other two, you're not doing it right. Globalism's expected negative consequences are even worse if you don't build all three legs. Simply put: people, money and machines must be free to go where they see the best opportunities, foreign borders and national identities be damned. Factories and capital respond well to the demands of globalism, they seem to move to where the best opportunities are. But, the third component, free movement of labor, is much trickier. In some circumstances, neoliberal policies fail because people don't like to move. And in other situations, when people do move, their migration creates other serious problems. Reconciling the theories of labor mobility with the realities of economic migration or lack thereof, is one of globalism's biggest challenges.

The European Union is a good example. They believe that open trade between their member countries, coupled with open capital flows and free migration of people is a net benefit for everyone. Thus, they have open borders internally for an area including four hundred million people, called the Schengen Area. If you're inside this zone, you can cross borders and travel unimpeded. Each year 1.3 billion people cross a border within the zone.

But terrorism and the migrant crisis of 2015-2017 forced countries to withdraw temporarily from the agreement, reimposing border controls and limiting travel.[44] The Paris terrorist attacks, which saw 130 people massacred, coupled with the massive Syrian migration, strained the borders and patience of many EU countries. The negative consequences of unfettered movement became too much to bear.

Now, the Europeans are rethinking their commitment to globalism and the open borders it demands. Some EU countries have had enough and are moving forward with greater caution. Not all of the countries are aligned, but they are talking and having a conversation about certain baseline assumptions they made, notably, whether or not to let people move freely throughout the EU. In fall 2017, Germany and France moved to extend their Schengen suspension for another two years. Terrorists have undoubtedly taken advantage of Schengen to move undetected within Europe, and countries will have to decide if the risk of future terrorist attacks is worth an idealized vision of open borders. Some countries like Poland and Hungary see a suspension of Schengen as necessary for preserving national identities. They don't want an influx of foreign migrants to alter the dynamics within their countries. The debate around open borders and free movement within the EU is volatile and each country has its own perspective, concerns, and agenda.

At home in the United States, we have our own issues. We've found that labor mobility doesn't work in the United States like it does in the text books. People like to stay where they are, enjoying their homes and communities despite dwindling economic opportunities. This surprised many economists. They assumed people would travel as long and far as they needed to find the next job or fledgling career. But people don't move when times get tough, they hunker down and hope for something new to arrive even though the odds of that happening are low. It's the poor and the working class who suffer the worst of it. Economist David Schleicher writes, "Cities that have economically declined due to increased trade competition from China have not seen matching declines in population, but instead have just had increases in unemployment."[45] Without perfect labor mobility, free trade and open capital movements can do more harm than good. When people say the rust belt has been hollowed out, this is what they mean. Free trade moved the factories, but the people stayed put.

Neoliberals and coastal elites don't like to talk about this problem because they lack the empathy required to appreciate the plight of the middle class. Your hometown factory closed? Oh well, get a new service job. That doesn't pay enough to live? Oh well, move somewhere cheaper or with better job prospects. Don't want to leave your family and community? Boy that's weird, what's a family and community?

The best example of elitist apathy towards the working class of America is when they waive off the consequences of globalism with a simple statement: find a new career. This is known as bootstrapping, or when an individual elects to overcome structural forces that are obstacles to success. The argument is that any one person can create a vibrant future for themselves if they would only apply their energy in a productive way. Right wingers have suggested marginalized or oppressed people of America could and should bootstrap their way over structural impediments on the road to productivity. Any failure to do so is a personal shortcoming. Progressives counter that argument by saying it ignores structural racism and/or oppressive institutions. They say it's impossible.

Yet, today, the Democratic left uses the very same argument against the white working class of America. The progressives say, hey poor unemployed factory worker, we know our open trade policies devoured your way of life, but why don't you just lift yourself by the bootstraps and get a new career? That's a dark, apathetic, and hypocritical viewpoint devoid of empathy and understanding. It divides the world into the sympathetic and the damned and the white working class abandoned by globalism are the ones left to fend for themselves, fumbling with useless bootstraps that won't help at all.

Coastal policy makers are often blinded by their own experiences. Many of the elite journalists, business people, and intellectuals who work in NYC, DC, and Silicon Valley moved there from elsewhere. These people have no roots where they live, no generational community. Most of them probably left their small town with pride, being one to escape their past and create a new lifestyle in the city. It's a self-selected population that cares more for personal achievement than community building. And now these people drive policy and media. It's no wonder they can't stand middle Americans who long for the old days, where family and community were most important.

Today's lifestyle of the urban elites is antithetical to the MAGA crowd and a large reason why so many Democrats ditched their party and went Deplorable. The arrogance and cold-hearted dissociation of Democrats from the heart of middle America was a fatal mistake. And their response to the ills of globalism is just one more way Deplorables felt the disdain and disregard emanating from big city politicians and policy makers. If Democrats' answer to the dying pleas of the American middle class is basically, "get over it," then it should be no surprise when millions of people erupt in revolt and elect a man like Donald Trump in response.

We all should have seen this pushback to globalism coming, but counter arguments and protests went unheeded. In 1999, the World Trade Organization met in Seattle for their annual meetings and the foreign dignitaries and global trade advocates who attended were met with an onslaught of protests that came to be known as the Battle in Seattle. But the anti-globalism messages were ignored. Rioters and protesters were ridiculed for being overly concerned with the idea that globalism would bring a "race to the bottom," where wages, labor practices, and environmental standards would converge upon the lowest common denominator. Their concerns were pushed aside with rubber bullets, tear gas, and mass arrests while the march towards neoliberal trade practices continued unabated.

But as it turns out, the Seattle protesters were right 20 years ago and they're still right today. Their predictions were prescient, clear, and should have been heeded. An article by Noah Smith in *The Atlantic* reflects:

> *"Economists David Autor, David Dorn, and Gordon Hanson did very careful empirical work and found that competition from China lowered wages and increased unemployment for American workers who were in competition with Chinese imports.*

> *Economists Michael Elsby, Bart Hobijn, and Aysegul Sahin found that competition from developing countries—not the decline of unions or the rise of automation—has been responsible for the bulk of the*

recent decline in labor's share of income in the United States."[46]

Bill Clinton, George W. Bush, and even Barack Obama all knew of the darker side of globalism, yet they each advanced the neoliberal trade agenda of open borders and free passage for products, capital, and people. They sacrificed the American middle class to the global order, eroding incomes, ending industries, and driving income inequality to all-time highs - despite the negative data being readily available. Almost two decades have passed since Seattle and we haven't deviated from the game plan despite losing every contest.

I

I HAVE A confession to make: I am a trained globalist myself. I attended one of the premier training grounds for globalist leaders in the entire world: The Georgetown University School of Foreign Service. I have a master's degree in international affairs and international finance with a regional focus on Latin America. There I learned about the globalist system from insiders, as Georgetown recruits some of the world's preeminent leaders as professors. I took classes with sitting Citibank Board Members, former White House Officials, and technocrats from the International Monetary Fund. They got their hooks in me and dumped the globalist dogma right down my throat, for which, I paid them handsomely in tuition.

Latin America was hot at the end of the '90s. Emerging Markets were sexy. Finance was increasingly sexy. I set out to become an international investment banker and applied to become a Hoya. The day Georgetown accepted my application, I ran over to campus and bought a coffee cup, already planning how I'd signal my pedigree at a future job. I was eager, excited, and naive.

In the year 2000, it's barely believable now, but the United States dusted off the Monroe Doctrine and started looking south for good times and opportunity. The Cold War was over, the big red threat was dead, and our gaze returned to the neighborhood. Latin America re-entered the consciousness. Bush promised a new trade zone, expanding NAFTA to the south pole, proposing the Free Trade Area of the Americas agreement. From southern Chile to northern Canada, the western hemisphere was to be become a powerhouse trade block to compete with the emergent European Union and rising China. The US had always claimed the west as our own, and it was time to tend the neglected garden. Businesses and academics declared Latin America as the next big thing. I missed the tech boom of the '90s and I didn't want to miss this. The future spoke Spanish and jetted off to Mexico City or Buenos Aires.

Now this is a side note to our main story but it is an interesting fact. The United States really was looking at home and in its backyard for the next big thing in the 1990s. Our view was sort of narrowing from the wide-angled global cold war focus to a real concentration on ourselves and our neighbors. When the Soviet Union collapsed and the Berlin Wall came down, it unleashed an energy which had been locked down for 50 years. The '90s were a Pax Americana. We cashed the peace dividend, ran budget surpluses, and even talked about when the national debt would be repaid. Bill Clinton didn't just balance budgets, the country was making money back then. Then the tech bubble started growing and the country felt rich. It seemed like everyone was making money, we had no enemies, and we drank in the victory over the evil communists. There may never be a decade like the golden era of the '90s. Part of this new world was to look south and refocus regionally rather than globally.

Then 9/11 happened while I was in graduate school. After a week of shock we returned to hear more bad news. Our own professor, who specialized in Latin America, who sold us on its importance, now took the lectern to share the unfortunate truth: the Latin American experiment is over. Your degrees are worthless. The new next big thing is Middle Eastern Studies. The $50,000 you spent? Flush it down the toilet. 9/11 whiplashed the national attention. Our focus had turned leisurely southward and was almost fixated, when suddenly Afghanistan and Iraq and Arabic snatched it up, and hasn't let go for almost 20 years. Latin America was relegated once again to forgotten cousin or weird neighbor status by an existential threat on the other side of the world. Instead of the new special relationship promised by George W. Bush, Latin America was now seen as source of national security threats to the United States.[47]

All this goes to show - this current bout of globalism may be temporary. If the United States can go from a cold war posture to a renewed Monroe Doctrine and then towards a focus on the Middle East, it can go from globalist, to regionalist, or even nationalist if circumstances demand it. Deplorable voters are almost universally opposed to a globalist set of priorities and voted for Trump in part because he promised to return our focus to America First. If the American middle class continues to feel the squeeze of globalization, if they still see their culture and community fade away into a vague promise of multiculturalism and an international perspective, they will persist in voting for people who hear their pleas. Donald Trump heard their cries and promised to help.

THE COLLEGE STUDENT IS PATIENT ZERO

W HEN IT CAME time to get into college, I didn't have many choices. I was a bad high school student. I'm not even sure I graduated, but the administrators gave me a social promotion and dumped me into the real world despite failing senior English. That you're reading about this in a book I've written is some delicious irony for my teachers, or much deserved congratulations for having the foresight to just get rid of me and let me figure things out on my own. At any rate, the college application process for me was fairly short. Suicide mission to the local commuter college, George Mason University, the suburban campus for suburban kids in Fairfax, Virginia.

I didn't really want to "be" anything at that point in my life, so philosophy seemed like the study of nothing and something at the same time. I chose it as my major and began reading. After Plato, Hobbes, Locke, and Rousseau I stumbled into a class all about Karl Marx. Some of it was over my head at the time, essays like, "On the Jewish Question" didn't have enough context for me, but his arguments on economics hit home. Labor product alienation, or the terrible feeling one gets cranking out work while all the benefits go to the factory owner, made sense. The reserve army of the unemployed also made sense. If the bad guys, capitalists, wanted to keep your wages down, having some unemployed dude standing by to take your job seemed like a smart ploy. But what really stuck was Marx's claim that the economic conditions of a time drive culture, society, and politics in a fundamental way. In fact, he believed economic conditions were the determining factor in all social and class relationships and how political relationships formed. To Marx, all questions could be answered with an examination of contemporary economic structures. I wanted to understand the world, and if Marx says economics determines everything, then adios philosophy, and hello economics. I knew I wasn't down with communism but Marx's use of economics as an analytical framework for understanding the world seemed interesting. I switched majors.

George Mason University's economic department is notoriously conservative. They fancied themselves a "little Chicago," positioning themselves second to the world famous(ly conservative) University of Chicago, home of Milton Friedman and Thomas Sowell among many other distinguished faculty. The free market, open borders, neo classical economics from Illinois became known as the Chicago School of Economics. The core philosophy of the Chicago School is that markets make better decisions than governments. They believed the open markets, made up of large groups of buyers and sellers of all things, would collectively make better decisions acting independently rather than relying on the government to decide everything. The Chicago School would rather sit back and allow individual preferences to express themselves in the marketplace rather than empower the government to make economic decisions on our behalf.

Some competing schools of thought believed the opposite, that the government should use its enormous power to drive the economy by making large purchases or investing in massive projects. The idea is, if the government spends enough money in just the right ways, everyone in the economy will benefit. This school of thought is called Keynesian Economics, after Maynard Keynes, and it was more commonly taught. In 1995 when I started undergrad, the Chicago School was mostly limited to the University of Chicago and good ole George Mason, where I happened to end up.

My accidental admittance to George Mason gave me an intellectual foundation in libertarianism and right-wing economic policies. I had no idea at the time these were radical ideas. The way the professors explained it, it was all just common sense and conventional wisdom. Looking back, it's clear many of the adjuncts used the lectern as a pulpit. Sure they educated us, but they were also looking for converts. They wanted to brainwash us, creating new adherents to their economic religion, ones who drank the dogma and shared the faith with others. I remember one professor explaining the origin of taxes with such fervor he'd pound his fist and let loose random spittle when the story crescendoed. The way he saw it, the birthplace of taxation was when some marauder realized it was more efficient to keep people alive and steal a little from them every year, rather than kill them right now and take everything they had. Not exactly a positive image. When delivered with sermon like passion, stories like this one nestled into my brain and helped create my mental model of the world. So today, when I hear Ben Shapiro say, "taxation is theft," his words already have a home in my mind. It just sort of clicks.

19 year old brains, like mine back then, aren't capable of defending themselves from mind invaders. They seem to be particularly receptive to ideas which help define the chaotic world teenagers are trying to figure out. Our brains are like open source computers, designed to receive instructions. Choosing a college is like selecting who will write the foundational code to perceive all future data. It's no exaggeration to say choosing a college is choosing how you will think for the rest of your life. College professors are the first people you really let get under the hood and tinker with your brain. High school is about prepping the circuitry, and college is where the real programming occurs.

I'll admit, studying economics at George Mason shaped my worldview. I easily see the libertarian, market-based argument for nearly any situation. My first inclination is liberty and freedom above all else. I'm loathe to consider government intervention in anything. If everyone would just leave each other alone, we'd all be a lot better off. In the economics department, my young mind was offered no alternative views, there was no fiery counter messaging offered by a young socialist, just a continuous indoctrination camp run by true believers desperate for more company.

I

THE SAME KIND of brainwashing is happening on campuses all over the country today. Kids think they're headed to college to get a broad-based understanding of the world but instead they end up becoming missionaries for a particular worldview. Except these days, the cult-curriculum isn't limited to specific classes on philosophy or economics. No, college culture begins the indoctrination before classes even start. Freshmen get the first wave in orientation when they're incapable of challenging authority or even aware there may be another point of view.

For example, in a student's first week at American University in Washington, DC, The Center for Diversity and Inclusion runs an orientation program. The program is meant to create a "more inclusive environment," which on the surface sounds ok enough. But the messaging students receive goes way beyond the goals of creating a welcoming campus life and delves straight into ideological transmission.

The school kicks off the orientation with the controversial and generally absurd notion that a student's gender may be anything other than male or female. They encourage students to identify themselves by saying "Hi, my name is ____ and my pronouns are ____." By introducing a sea of gender and pronoun choices to wide-eyed 18 year olds at orientation, the school slides a preposterous assumption into the daily discourse on campus: biological science is irrelevant. Even if new gender identities are a real thing (which they are not), the science on this matter is hardly settled. Gender identity expansion is a radical idea which should be considered with scrutiny, not just hand delivered to baby-faced teenagers as settled truth. This identification procedure is also an example of language control, whereby one student can demand the other use specific words when addressing them or else face the consequences.

Then the Center for Diversity and Inclusion tells all incoming freshmen they each have unconscious biases which must be uncovered and redirected.[48] The university administration explains that despite whatever overt behavior students have exhibited their entire lives, deep inside each of these college freshmen is a racist or sexist which must be extinguished. This notion is presumably based on the Implicit Association Test, which claims an ability to suss out your inherent racism through a quick test. And although it is quite popular with Diversity people and Human Resources departments, this test is widely seen as flawed, damaged, and even harmful.[49] Subjecting students to assumptions (you're all racists) developed from a failed science experiment is an obvious example of ideology trumping reason. Orientation to campus life is mostly an orientation to a religion rather than to objectivity.

Later in the same discussion, the presenters explain how other people's feelings are your responsibility. They assert that students are held accountable for how other people respond to things they say, irrespective of the speaker's intent. The listener's emotional reaction is all that matters. As a child I was taught, "Sticks and stones may break my bones but words will never hurt me," but at American University they now teach that words can and do hurt, and whoever speaks bad words is a bad person. The rationality or reasonableness of the listener's reaction is irrelevant. Only their emotions matter.

As if all this wasn't a lot to digest in one day, then the Title IX office comes out to share the sexual assault policy. The presenters explain, among many other things, "A student who has experienced sexual violence will never be required to participate in an investigation process at AU."[50] At American University, no one who accuses a person of sexual violence will have to answer even the most basic questions about the alleged event. Accusers are assumed to be honest in all cases, that they somehow were born without the ability to lie. The most basic civil liberties we have in America, such as the right to face an accuser, are abandoned at the campus gates and in their place new draconian procedures are inserted which appear to assume an accused person's guilt.

In a student's first afternoon at college, they are introduced to several key components of the new leftist platform:

1. You are a racist.

2. Words make victims.

3. Feelings trump science.

4. Victims are beyond scrutiny.

That's quite a lot to digest in your first week. Also, there seems to be a lot of bad things happening at school. Words, pronouns, unconscious biases, and sexual assault all reign terror on campus and (almost) everyone is a potential victim.

I say *almost* because someone must be doing all this victimizing. A quick look at the Center for Diversity and Inclusion's website offers a hint of just who the campus perpetrators may be. Their tag line is: "Enhancing LGBTQ, Multi-cultural, First-Generation, and Women's Experiences on Campus."

Who are they protecting? Let's see. Women? Check. People of color? Check. Gay and lesbian? Check. Even immigrants, check. Well, who does that leave out as the bad guy?

Straight white American men. Welcome to college, boys.

The Center for Diversity and Inclusion is an administrative office staffed with professionals hired by the University. This is not a student club, or some renegade pack of radicals. The orientation sessions are part of the official school policy. It's easy to dismiss bad ideas and stupid behavior found on college campuses by assuming it's the fault of wild misguided kids. But in reality, it is the administrations who are cultivating and tolerating an environment where students are taught through overt statements and subtle messaging that white American men are the oppressors and everyone else are their victims. And you don't even have to actually oppress anyone anymore to be a bad guy, people just get to say you made them *feel* oppressed, and boom, you're a monster. An individual's feelings have been elevated above facts and reason as the sole arbiter of truth.

The ideas pushed by the Title IX office and the Center for Diversity and Inclusion have a philosophical and ideological foundation called intersectionality. If you haven't heard about it by now, you will soon enough as intersectionality is marching through our universities and into our institutions. It drives policy, changes the nature of human interaction, and feeds the culture war in America. You can see it's direct influence on presentations like the one from the Center for Diversity and Inclusion. They claim to protect every other identity group besides straight white guys and feed victim culture by creating new ways to be oppressed. The cultural divide which results from intersectionality had a direct impact on the election in 2016 and is partially why Donald Trump got elected.

II

INTERSECTIONALITY IS A feminist mutation. After feminism earned women full civil rights and equality under the law, feminist theory evolved to find greater purpose. Like a restless army after a decisive victory, the feminist machinery sought out new conflicts to keep things rolling. Institutions built for conflict don't simply dissipate upon victory, they reorient their cause and identify new battlegrounds. So the theory metastasized beyond civil rights for women and filtered into every minority's relationship with the world. Kimberle Crenshaw, a feminist academic, is credited with defining the term in her paper, "Demarginalizing the Intersection of Race and Sex: A Black Feminist Critique of Anti-discrimination Doctrine, Feminist Theory, and Antiracist Politics," written in 1989. There she explains how white women can't speak for black women on feminist issues, because white women are ignorant of the black female's lived experience.

Intersectionality is meant to address oppression on a more specific level than just gender by accounting for multiple avenues of oppression beyond being female. Handicapped black women have a different oppression experience than say, a gay Latino male. A poor Indian woman is oppressed differently than a gender-fluid bi-sexual biracial person, and most importantly a rich white woman has little to no understanding of the oppression experienced by anyone else. Some of this seems logical, understanding a person's specific circumstances could help inform possible remedies.

But, overall the extended application of intersectional-ity is divisive and tribal. Because women have resolved their civil rights claims, to remain "oppressed" they must identify with narrowing definitions of self. The outcome is an ever tightening cordon separating people based on specific identities. At its core, intersectionality is atomizing rather than uniting. Feminism, and now intersectionality, isn't about bringing people together, it's about separation and conflict. This conflict has two fronts. The first is where oppressed peoples compete for victim status among themselves. And the second is when they blame the only group capable of oppression for their problems. Unsurprisingly, Crenshaw explains which group has that power when she says, "white and male privilege is implicit and understood."

An analysis of Google search shows interest intersectionality and white male privilege exploded around 2012. Searches for the word feminism have also increased dramatically since then. All three subjects occupy more of the national conversation than ever before. For some reason, America's focus turned towards white male privilege and intersectional theory after years of disinterest. Crenshaw first wrote about this back in the '80s after all. But now it's as if the country suddenly enacted a new national policy, zeroing in on the evil white male and all the ways he harms everyone else. While it's impossible to narrow it down, the rise of identity politics under Obama and the explosion of intersectionality seem inextricably linked, each feeding the other, together creating a new cultural environment, one which sorts the country into two groups: the oppressive white American Male, and everyone else, his victims.

III

LET'S STEP BACK for a minute, it's important to consider the context. Imagine you're 18 years old. Your parents, teachers, counselors, mentors, media, culture, and everyone else has been telling you your entire life college is the only way to success. Everything you did in high school was to improve your chances of attending the best college. There has never been a vision of your future life that didn't include a college degree. Despite the incredible and ever increasing cost of tuition, the future years of debt, the handcuffs of financial obligations clamped around the wrists of youth, you believe attending college is not just smart, but really the only option. Avoiding college is like shirking a great responsibility and honor. Fighting against the idea of college is to battle with cultural mythology and group expectations. Few can resist. So when you arrive on campus in that first week, nervous and excited, without the support of your high school friends and family, all alone for the first time in your life in a strange place with strange people, where suddenly you're an adult with adult-like options, in a place you've dreamed about and idealized, it's no crazy thing to say, you're open to suggestions.

In the old days, the dogma was limited to the classroom. Instructors displayed their biases during lectures and when grading papers. Your brain got washed while learning economics or philosophy, not when you went to orientation. The subject matter may have been biased but the administration assumed we were decent human beings and before classes started all we needed to learn was where the library was. Today, the administrations start with a different assumption, one that believes humanity is dark, one that sees hate and oppression everywhere, one that sees boys as rapists, and victims...victims are everywhere.

Orientation isn't about orienting to student life, but rather a crash course in the culture war. After a week on campus, you know which side of that war you're on. Intersectionality tells you so. Over here we have the people of color, the women, the LGBTQ, the immigrants, the handicapped..and over there are cis gendered heterosexual masculine white males and the women who love them. The oppressed vs. the oppressor. Good vs. bad. Light vs. evil. Life vs. death. Intersectionality cannot exist without an antagonist. It depends on maintaining and nurturing a foil. If you've wondered why there seems to be a resurgence in hatred, this is why. Without hate, intersectionality has no reason to exist.

These ideas spiral outwards from colleges and into society. Universities are the petri dishes of culture, where concepts and perspectives are born, some positive and some pernicious. Theories fester into practice, inserting themselves into impressionable minds who then spill out into the world infecting every institution they later inhabit. The epidemiology of ideas identifies the college freshman as patient zero and as they criss cross the country after graduation, the infected spread whatever viral ideology they contracted on campus and the nation feels it.

This infection is a primary reason why Democrat to Deplorable is happening. College students become young professionals and in time they become leaders. The organizations which recruit graduates adapt to and accept the ideas kids bring with them. Policies based on ideas of implicit bias and pervasive oppression become required baselines as colleges deliver wave after wave of indoctrinated graduates to the real world. Institutional take over starts at the ground level and corporations and the governments who hire people must adapt to the demands of the recent college graduates. There is a direct connection from ideology based education policies, to corrupted graduates, and ultimately to the rapid evolution of the adult universe in response. Simply put, colleges are exporting hate to the world.

Democrat to Deplorable voters have had enough.

91.8% of Democrat to Deplorable voters agree or strongly agree with the following statement: "I am concerned about the state of affairs on college campus."

IV

How DID WE get here? Eight years after the joy of electing our first black president, racial tensions only worsened. Despite the nation uniting to shatter the black ceiling, today we seem more divided than before. The tone of the country soured and so has the discourse emanating from our universities. How did the atmosphere on college campus suddenly change? Why did interest in intersectionality and white male privilege explode around 2011-2012? While it's impossible to determine exactly, something did happen then which transformed the university experience and forced these issues to the forefront.

In 2011, Barack Obama's administration wanted to update a 40 year old federal law called Title IX, originally created to ensure boys and girls had equal access to college programs like sports. Title IX was a victory for the old feminism, a righteous one which sought to bring parity between males and females and end gender-based discrimination. The law protected women's rights to education, ensuring equity among the sexes. The key section:

No person in the United States shall, on the basis of sex, be excluded from participation in, be denied the benefits of, or be subjected to discrimination under any education program or activity receiving federal financial assistance. (Title IX of the Education Amendments of 1972.)

Born out of the civil rights era, Title IX granted women the same educational opportunities as men and enshrined their rights as laws. The government mandated compliance through their enforcement division, the Office of Civil of Rights. If the OCR found schools guilty of non-compliance, they could revoke federal funding and cripple the school's program. The threat of financial ruin is powerful and the schools responded. They worked to provide a discrimination free experience for women who then took advantage. Women now outnumber men on campus 3:2 and earn more degrees than their male counterparts. By all accounts the law was a success.

Then everything changed in 2011.

At the time, a new moral panic had swept the nation. Researchers released a study that claimed one in four women on campus were victims of sexual violence. 1 in 4. 25%. The numbers are staggering. On a normal sized campus of 10,000 students, with 6,000 women, this meant 1,500 were victims. If you just looked around the dining hall, there would be countless survivors. Everyone would know someone who was subjected to the disgusting crime of sexual violence. The Obama administration and Joe Biden in particular were disturbed by these numbers. They were shocked to learn about this epidemic crushing the souls of our nation's young women. Once they learned of the rapist armies roaming across the universities, they decided something had to be done. Action had to be taken to save our girls from sexual predators.

The Obama administration issued an update to the Title IX laws. They sent a "Dear Colleague Letter" (DCL) to every school which received federal funding. In the DCL, Obama demanded schools update their Title IX policies to focus on solving the rape crisis. The rape culture which had been allowed to bloom on campus had to be destroyed. The DCL cited the "one in four" sexual violence number as their motivation and now schools were obligated to solve this problem or else lose their funding.

As you can imagine, this brought many aggressive changes, including some which stepped on standard civil rights endowed to all Americans. Victims were encouraged to come forward under the protection of anonymity. Title IX officers became judge, jury, and executioner, by hearing *and* adjudicating student complaints. And in an effort to capture as many rapists as possible, the Obama administration reduced the standard of evidence used to determine guilt down to just a preponderance of evidence. Because this issue was so critical, a campus tribunal could find a perpetrator guilty if there was just a 50.01% chance he did it. We had to save our daughters. Lower standards of guilt meant less rapists would get away.

Schools and the OCR worked together to push policies even beyond the guidelines. As the OCR cracked down on offending schools, the federal agency would negotiate more expansive policies intent on solving the crisis. When these cases were settled, the agreements became public and set new standards. Obama's OCR systemically raised the temperature on schools, and in turn they cracked down harder on campus.

Ultimately, a new industry was born. New offices, new requirements, new policies, new administrators, new trainings, new mandates. Schools had to root out evil and spread the good word. They recruited everyone to achieve their aims. Anyone who touched campus life in any way was now the eyes and ears of the University. Title IX offices set up new reporting systems, encouraged secret tips, and ensured anonymity. The federal government didn't just require schools to respond to complaints, recipients of federal education funding had to proactively prevent anything bad from happening at all.

Schools protected victims in ways never before seen. Victims would never be challenged. The standard for conviction was lowered. Students were deputized to report on each other through anonymous tip lines. Normal civil liberties were pushed to the side in favor of safety and security for women.

The threat was just that real.

Or was it?

In reality, the entire Title IX apparatus born out of the 2011 DCL is based on a fabrication. The Obama administration used a flawed survey which has been debunked numerous times.[51][52] Even the authors of the study themselves said it wasn't nationally representative and was inappropriate for generalizations about colleges in the US. It was advocacy propaganda falling far short of any scientific standards. It was a survey with poor response rates. The terms were redefined to expand the potential pool of victims. Basically, anything women didn't like about men was included as sexual violence to inflate the numbers. Yet despite the flawed science, the Obama administration seized upon it to promote their agenda.

The feds were either insanely stupid or willingly ignorant when they cited this study as cause to expand Title IX and radically alter the environment on campus, but cite it they did, and the study became the basis for sweeping changes.

The alleged rape statistics don't even pass the sniff test much less a basic analysis. One in four women at American University would mean 1,250 instances of sexual violence occurred at AU alone. A quick google search of American University's self-reported statistics show 18 rape and five "fondling" reports filed at AU in 2015.[53] These aren't prosecutions or even convictions, just accusations. 18 rape accusations is 18 too many, but in the context of 5,000 undergraduate women on campus, it's 0.36% of the female population. If I counted the grad students, the rate would be even lower. The reality painted by real statistics does not match with the paranoia.

Rape is obviously a terrible crime, but does it really rise to the level of a national crisis? Do American women face the same dangers at college as women in Sierra Leone or in war zones where rape is weaponized for political and genetic gains? If one in four American women are raped at college, parents must ask themselves if a liberal education is worth a good shot their daughter will be violated by a ruthless rapist or at least by her drunken privileged not-really-boyfriend-we're-just-talking fling for the week. If the statistics are to be believed, and they are by the federal government and university administrators, American parents are sadistic and ruthless. Casting your daughter into a den of rapists seems like a cold move, even if the larger goal is a mediocre education and 20 years of student loan debt. A sobering thought, if true. Nevertheless, the government is a believer. Title IX became even more powerful after 2011 and expanded relentlessly into 2017.

As regulations tend to do, Title IX has mutated and exploded into a grotesque distortion of its original goals. The 2011 DCL Title IX guidance was expanded even further in 2013 when the government redefined harassment to include "unwelcome" verbal communication. Now the federal government even regulates people's feelings, too. As Emily Yoffe, a contributing editor to *The Atlantic* wrote,

> *"Title IX is now a cudgel with which the government and school administrators enforce sex rules too bluntly, and in ways that invite abuse. That's an uncomfortable statement."*[54]

It's hard to overstate the impact of these policies. Title IX was the key which turned on the machinery of victim culture, and that machine gnarled campus life and eventually the country. The Title IX DCL is an astounding example of how bureaucratic changes tied to money have a multiplier effect which ripple outwards from the stroke of a pen into the relationships and human interactions which collectively define our society. It is a dark and sobering reminder of big government's influence on our children and a vivid example of why less is more when it comes to regulation.

Whether Obama hoped for the secondary consequences or they were simply unforeseen is debatable, but whether or not they had an impact is certain. Schools feared losing billions of dollars in federal funding and in turn cracked down on a fabricated enemy. That truth, reality, independent agency, civil liberties, and a healthy adult perspective are collateral damage, seemed irrelevant.

V

SADLY, COLLEGES AREN'T just producing misguided young adults, they're making the kids mentally ill. Yes, college students are taught to be depressed, anxious, and paranoid at the same time they're studying literature or biology. Rather than teach our children how to handle the rigors of the real world, colleges, under threats by the federal government, are turning them into fragile collections of outrage held together only by a quest to avenge an oppressor.

Greg Lukianoff and Jonathan Haidt's seminal essay, *"The Coddling of The American Mind,"* explains the current campus culture in terms of mental health.[55] They believe the universities are teaching our children to be sick rather than strong, that the tools the administration are dispensing don't strengthen and fortify, but rather erode emotional foundations resulting in a new wave of depression, anxiety, and normalized mentally ill behavior. In their article, they compare the directives of university administrators, Title IX officers, and overzealous campus activists to the tenets of cognitive behavioral therapy (CBT) and find the adults are encouraging the kids to be sick.

CBT is a powerful form of self-help, a drug-free way to ease depression and anxiety by changing the way you think. It teaches you to acknowledge damaging thinking and helps you to redirect your thoughts into something more realistic and positive. According to Lukianoff and Haidt, CBT is the "embodiment of ancient wisdom" and proven to be more useful and effective than drugs in treating a wide range of mental disorders. The basic idea of CBT is this: once you identify distorted thinking, you can change it and in turn you can control your emotions.

One of the first things students are taught on campus is that the emotions of a listener are more important than the facts or truth of what was said. In CBT, this is called emotional reasoning. Using emotions to guide thinking is the opposite of a healthy behavior. CBT teaches you to identify thinking like this and turn it around. But student life on campus teaches the opposite. It codifies the emotional state of the listener as the most important reality and creates an ecosystem around this idea, encouraging students to report each other to Bias Response Teams or the Title IX offices. Rather than discourage what 12-step programs call "stinking thinking," colleges now teach kids to double down on their perceived angst. Surely, some ideas are offensive and should be taken that way, but to construct an objective reality based on an individual's emotional response is a path to madness.

Lukianoff and Haidt explain several more components of CBT in their article and relate each back to the college climate, drawing a straight line from school policies to student mental health. From trigger warnings, to safe spaces, to controlled speech, and a focus on personal 'trauma' - Universities are doing the exact opposite a therapist would recommend. Teaching students biased or ideologically based academics is one thing, but encouraging them to be sick is another. It's a reasonable question to ask, are we doing more harm than good?

Title IX paranoia, intersectionality, and a focus on emotional reasoning combine not just to change the way people think and act, but now this whole twisted dance is creating a new system of moral values. Jonathan Haidt has been following all of this closely and he suggests the college climate is creating a new moral system based on victimhood rather than dignity or honor. He writes:

"The new moral culture of victimhood fosters 'moral dependence' and an atrophying of the ability to handle small interpersonal matters on one's own. At the same time that it weakens individuals, it creates a society of constant and intense moral conflict as people compete for status as victims or as defenders of victims."[56]

A victim culture doesn't confer value to acts of honor or dignity but rather to those who are the most aggrieved. Instead of competing to see who can be the most honorable or dignified, the race is to become the most oppressed or discriminated. In this setting, dominance becomes the most egregious moral violation, as those with power are the only ones capable of oppression. The moral culture evolves to encourage a divisive competition for oppressed status, and a unifying opposition to power, real or imagined. Finding and naming what oppresses you becomes the easiest path to higher status and moral value. A winner in victim culture is best attuned to slights, offense, and oppression and then able to translate that into attention and power.

Haidt continues,

"This is the great tragedy: the culture of victimization rewards people for taking on a personal identity as one who is damaged, weak, and aggrieved. This is a recipe for failure -- and constant litigation -- after students graduate from college and attempt to enter the workforce."

Ironically, a victim culture is most likely to occur in societies with high levels of diversity and equality. When a culture's power hierarchy becomes flatter, it takes less 'oppression' to trigger outrage. As the United States becomes even more diverse, we can expect higher levels of outrage at smaller and smaller offenses. And in this light, Universities with their expansive diversity programs are a logical place to see victim culture take hold. It's discouraging to think greater diversity may mean greater conflict and the fetishization of victimhood. But this appears to be the course we are on. And it won't just stay on campus; eventually this moral code will expand into our institutions and politics, changing the fundamental ways we interact and the very fabric of our nation.

Democrat to Deplorable voters are tuned in to this phenomenon.

According to my survey, 71% of respondents agreed, "The emergence of victim culture motivated me to vote in 2016."

VI

IT'S NOT A great leap to see the connection here between victim culture, intersectionality, and Title IX. Intersectionality provides an ideological framework to seek victim status and what emerges is a culture based on victimhood, where people are incentivized to find insult and oppression, rather than opportunities for strength or dignity. Words became weapons. Ideas became assault. Offense became discrimination. Where in the past, offensive words were shrugged off by remembering 'sticks and stones...' today they become reasons for filing complaints.

Kids used to resolve their conflicts among themselves, if someone insulted or offended you, you could confront them or shrug it off. People were empowered to handle their own affairs, especially when it came to how they felt.

We owned our emotions and accepted responsibility for managing them.

But the emergent victim culture now bestows power to those who are the most aggrieved. The Title IX apparatus institutionalizes such behavior, formalizing it as a normal way of life. The DCL forced Universities to eradicate bad think and prevent students from being offended, or else they'd lose their federal funding.

The result: a new generation of mentally ill young adults is turned lose on America, taught to become victims rather than heroes, emotional rather than logical, and dependent rather than self-sufficient.

The University system and its filthy cynical dance with the federal government and politics was why former Democrats who went to college, those who value higher education, who once believed college was the answer to every problem, were then fed up with the system and voted to drop a Trump Bomb on Washington, DC. If Andrew Breitbart was right when he said politics are downstream from culture, and I'm right when I say culture is downstream from college, campuses are one of the most important fronts in the current culture war. And absent significant changes, things at Universities are only going to deteriorate. Until college life changes, the culture war will rage on and the polarization of politics will continue.

At the time of publication it appears the Trump administration is trying to solve some of these issues. In mid-2017, Betsy DeVos, Trump's education secretary, rescinded the 2011 Dear Colleague Letter and announced the guidance contained therein would undergo public comment and modification, something the original never did. Obama's administration force-fed the colleges new policies, by-passing long-established procedures for stakeholders and concerned citizens, something entirely antithetical to an open society. And now Trump's team will open the floor for comment, bringing the sanitizing effect of open discussion and analysis to something not only crazy on its face, but crazy making in its effect. For those who saw Trump as a path out of the chaos and into the light, remedying the Title IX crisis and restoring a culture of sanity will be a massive victory. To me, if he fixes this alone, then it will all be worth it.

ANTI-FEMINIST BUT PRO-WOMAN

HILLARY CLINTON'S VAGINA was the centerpiece of her campaign. When she chose "I'm with HER" as her rallying cry, Clinton left little doubt about her most distinguished Presidential qualification. Because she promised four more years of the Obama administration, she set herself apart through constant reference to her genitals, gender, and sexual identity. Through careful consideration and deliberate action, Hillary became the Queen of Feminism. Her march to the White House was to be feminism's capstone accomplishment. At long last, a woman would break through the glass ceiling and become the most powerful person in the world.

A vote for Clinton was a vote for feminism's final victory over oppressive male power. A vote against her was a plea to remain in the patriarchy. She narrowed the world into a 'with us or against us' mindset. Good people over here with the Queen of Feminism, and the bad people over there with the darkness of male domination. Good vs. Evil. Light vs. Dark. Right vs. Wrong. It was a simple binary decision. A purposeful dichotomy, one which cleaved the nation into good girls and bad guys. In doing so, Clinton doubled down on the gender issue and became a feminist scion. She owned it. This was her moment. This was their moment.

Presumably, Clinton thought this was a smart electoral strategy. Her campaign must have believed they would find enough solidarity with other feminists to win the primary and eventually the general election. Surely they did poll testing, surveys, and market analysis which told them a feminist campaign, complete with a gender-related slogan and constant references to becoming the first woman President would be a winner. When Clinton tied herself to the feminist movement, she must have believed its historic momentum would help carry her over the finish line.

But what Clinton and her team were unable to see was that today's feminism has mutated into something incomprehensible. It's now devolved away from its earlier noble efforts and into something pernicious, chaotic, and divisive. Clinton's old age and isolation from the real America may explain this blind spot. The feminism of Clinton's youth was more about civil rights and women in the workplace, rather than the assault on reason and science it's become today.

Ironically, had Clinton run on a feminist campaign in the '90s or '00s, contemporary events may have helped her rather than hurt her as they did in 2016. Back then feminism was about getting equal rights and reasonable protections for women, something we all agree was a good thing. But today's feminism is a twisted cancer and people who support women's rights can find themselves at odds with current feminist practices. People like me. In the 1990s, the ugly side of feminist overreach had not yet revealed itself to the country, whereas in 2016, large swaths of the US were feeling the dissonance of new feminist thinking. Clinton, being a decade or two late, failed to see how adopting a feminist brand brought a cadre of downsides that were not due to "misogyny" as she would later claim, but instead owed to her assumption of a toxic ideology that alienates more than it liberates.

While Clinton and her team missed this crucial point, Democrat to Deplorable voters did not. To us, feminism and gender politics are not rallying cries but rather ominous signs of subversion and division. Another step towards a feminist utopia would be one more towards undermining our society and culture at large, something the feminists desire and Deplorables fear. Make America Great Again became the counterbalance to I'm with HER, and the dividing lines were set: Trump's red MAGA hats on one side and Clinton's pink vagina hats on the other. Anti-feminists vs. Feminists. Order vs. Chaos. Reality vs. Fantasy.

62% of Democrat to Deplorable voters strongly agree or agree with: "Fighting back against feminism motivated me to vote in the election."

Only 16% disagree/strongly disagree.

I

IN TODAY'S POLARIZED climate, our degraded discourse often forces people into all or nothing positions. Either you believe in man-made climate change and we must do everything we can to stop it, or you're a climate denier. Black Lives Matter or Blue Lives Matter. Unfettered immigration or you're a xenophobe. There's little room for ideas like, maybe we do have an impact on the climate, but are you sure the predictive models are correct? Or, yes it's a tragedy when a police officer shoots a black man, but why do black men kill each other at a much higher rate and why aren't we talking about that too? Or surely infinite immigration is bad, so what exactly should the quota be?

There is a severe shortage of thinkers who can carry in their head competing thoughts or ideas which appear to be contradictory, even if careful consideration reveals them to be logically consistent. Physicist Eric Weinstein calls these "long-short positions," alluding to investment strategies with multiple parts which when considered individually appear to be going in different directions, but in fact, are operating on the same thesis. When people engage in long-short thinking, zealots react with rage and try to box you into one position or the other. It's as if they can't handle the issue's complexity and instead respond with emotional outbursts.

And when it comes to feminism and women, it's precisely the same. Either you believe in feminism and all its goals, or you're a misogynistic woman hater. Nuance is a lost art today, so what I'm about to say might be hard for some people to understand: *you can be anti-feminist yet pro-woman.*

I have some incredible women in my life. My sister was a firefighter, a police officer, and served in Iraq. My mother changed careers in middle age to become a Doctor and run a prestigious emergency medicine department. I'm immensely proud of them both. They exercised choice and independence earned for them by the original feminist movement, and for that I'm grateful. Once upon a time, women couldn't vote, couldn't get credit cards, bank loans, or have an independent life separate from a husband. But all that has changed. The original feminist wars were righteous and necessary. America is the land of the free after all, and women deserve as much as freedom as anyone else.

But what's happening today isn't your grandmother's feminism. It's no longer about equality under the law or equal opportunity at work, school, or life. No, feminism today has evolved beyond a civil rights movement and into a new religion, a religion that requires an abandonment of science, a rejection of objectivity, and a denial of observable reality. Feminism isn't about changing the laws anymore; it's about changing the very nature of our existence.

But before we get into how feminism distorts reality and wishes to destroy the essence of our society, I want to make one distinction. There are many branches of feminism's family tree and not all of them are insane. I identify as an equity feminist, which means I believe that women should have all the same protections and rights under the law as anyone else, they should have equal opportunities as the rest of us, and the freedom to make the choices they wish – even if those decisions make other women mad. Equity feminism also means that I am open to the evolving research and science regarding men and women and I'll follow the data wherever it goes. Steven Pinker, the Harvard University evolutionary psychologist and best-selling author, defines equity feminism as "a moral doctrine about equal treatment that makes no commitments regarding open empirical issues in psychology or biology."[57] Other leading equity feminists are Camille Paglia and Christina Hoff Sommers. They each share common beliefs: Women should have the same rights and protections as men. But they also acknowledge that men and women are different, with different preferences and desires, and those preferences will lead to different outcomes. To me this all seems perfectly sane, but to many others, like gender feminists, what Paglia, Sommers, and Pinker believe is blasphemy. So when I'm critical of feminism in this book, it is not directed towards the equity feminists, but rather the gender feminists, Marxist feminists, intersectional feminists and so on.

II

WOMEN'S STANDING IN society has quietly overtaken men's. Feminism will have you believe women are oppressed and maligned, tortured by male power, and forced into submission to the patriarchy. If you merely listen to the headlines and feminist advocates, you may still believe women are at a disadvantage relative to men today.

But the state of women in 2017 hardly reflects an oppressed class of people. If women were oppressed by a dominating male patriarchy, then women would earn less money, be less educated, be unhealthier, less wealthy, and ultimately die faster and more frequently than men, right? Oppression is serious business, and what is the point of oppressing a class of people if you can't 'keep them down?'

But a look at the data shows women are outpacing men across some vital statistics. Young women fare far better than their young male counterparts in grade school.[58] This leads to higher high school graduation rates for women than men.[59] More women get into college, and more women earn degrees.[60] Then, women out-earn their male counterparts in professional jobs in 147 of the top 150 cities in the United States.[61] More women advance to managerial roles than men do.[62] And ultimately they end up controlling more wealth.[63] Along the way women are less likely to die at work, less likely to suffer from alcohol and drug abuse, and predictably, live longer lives than men.[64][65][66] So not only are women getting better educations, making more money, holding more managerial positions, and controlling more wealth, but they also live longer healthier lives at the same time. But you never hear about this from feminists or the media and government they control, do you?

Today, the truth is, women learn more, earn more, have better health and control more wealth than men. It hardly seems possible given the constant rhetoric about male oppression, rape culture, the wage gap, and all the terrible things women were protesting in January 2017 during the Women's March on DC. With pink pussy hats on their heads, women descended into Washington to protest the wretched state of affairs for American females. Maybe they are willfully ignorant or brainwashed themselves, but the reality is women today are freer, healthier, wealthier, better educated, and more secure than ever before.

If there is systemic oppression in our society, wouldn't the stats bear it out? How does the patriarchy benefit men when women seem to be winning in every meaningful category? It's almost as if the constant harping on the wage gap and male oppression is meant to cover up the real truth: men are falling behind in every measurable way. It seems feminists are not only winning their war against men, but they are also winning the information war as well. If the truth were well known, feminists would lose their standing and their entire industry would fall apart. In its place would appear a national effort to save our men from declining education, declining wage performance, depression, and suicide. These are the real data points for oppression. As you examine the facts, the idea our society colludes to marginalize females in favor of men evaporates under the heat of inspection. The patriarchy is the foundational myth of feminism, without it, feminism dies and the ideology which underpins the national narrative crumbles.

Democrat to Deplorable voters understand this. They see it with their own two eyes; they live it every day. Feminists escape reality by being willingly blind, whereas the anti-feminist yet pro-female Democrat to Deplorable voters remain grounded. So when Hillary Clinton takes on the mantle of feminism and proclaims her march to the Presidency is the final victory of feminism over the patriarchy, those who value reality over illusions, order over chaos, and truth over fiction are going to rebel. Donald Trump was our last ditch effort to save reality from a lie.

III

In October 2017, the highly respected global news magazine, *The Economist,* printed an article titled, "Why do women still earn a lot less than men?" Given that the wage gap issue remains one of the preferred tools of division by the feminist left, it was easy to assume the article would be filled with erroneous data pushing the myth that men and women get paid differently for the same jobs. Instead, I was pleasantly surprised when I read this striking confession, "According to data from 25 countries, gathered by Korn Ferry, a consultancy, women earn 98% of the wages of men who are in the same roles at the same employers."

While I knew the wage gap was fiction, I wasn't expecting the Economist to admit it. The wage gap myth is a prominent tool of disinformation promulgated by the left, including Obama, Clinton, and every single disingenuous politician looking to score points with feminists and their supporters. The baseline assumption of the wage gap idea is that somewhere in corporate America, a human resources staffer is making an explicit decision, "This woman is just as qualified as the man, but around here, we don't pay women as much as men, so she's only going to get 77% of what we pay the guys." That single instance of misogyny is then replayed millions of times across each industry and the entire nation, until the cumulative effect is that women are paid 3/4 of what men are.

What a haunting specter this is, a coordinated effort among hiring managers to pay women lower wages and force them into poorer economic conditions solely for the sake of oppressing females. This horror terrifies women and their supporters, unites them in the face of male oppression, and justifies the ongoing evolution of feminist theory. If our culture won't pay women the same as men, if it actively works to oppress women in 2018, then the war's conclusion is beyond the horizon and today's battles are as important as ever. The wage gap is a rallying cry for the restless feminist army. It is the banner they fly as they engage in day-to-day degradation of the male patriarchy.

What is the patriarchy? To feminists, every society has been male-dominated, every male-dominated society has oppressed women, and the society we live in today continues to dominate and oppress women, as evidenced by the wage gap, unfair hiring practices, and rape culture. Men control every aspect of society starting with the government, business, social institutions, local politics, and even the family. Male power is reinforced through law, social structures, mores, norms, philosophy, literature, and even science. A reliance on objectivity and rationality is preferred by male thinkers, and therefore sexist. Men control everything and in doing so, control women. Or so the theory goes.

As I read more of the Economist article, I began to realize this wasn't the 'end of the wage gap' story I was hoping it to be. Instead of accepting their first data point as the conclusion, that 98% of women earn the same as men for the same job, the writer segued into complaining that too many women are concentrated in jobs that pay less than men. The issue is no longer that men get paid more for the same work, but now it's that men take jobs which pay more than women do. The Economist explains how women tend to congregate in industries such as education, healthcare, and secretarial work which pay less than male-dominated industries like technology and finance. It also explains how 45-75% of women elect to work fewer hours when they have children, preferring to be at home with the babies rather than hustling in the workplace. And far fewer men report being stay at home dads or elementary school teachers than women do.

Rather than conclude their argument by explaining how men and women are different, with different biological realities, different expectations for themselves, different dispositions, and different risk appetites - the Economist article wraps up with a pithy summary which encapsulates all that is wrong the feminist movement today, "Gender equality will remain elusive until boys are as excited as girls about becoming teachers, nurses and full-time parents."

Read that again. Equality will be impossible until "boys are as excited as girls about becoming teachers, nurses, and full-time parents." Equality cannot exist while boys and girls are excited and motivated by different things. Therefore, equality demands boys and girls desire precisely the same things, in all circumstances, from now and forever. Simply put, feminism will not rest until boys become girls. This is the real goal of feminists today. It's not to gain women civil rights, they've already done that. It's not to get women independence, as this too is already complete. And it's not even to crush the wage gap, because as admitted above, the wage gap has already been demolished. The final goal of feminism is to eradicate masculinity, male interests, male spaces, and ultimately, erase maleness entirely from our society. How else can feminists claim victory over the patriarchy if not by destroying the very thing which creates it?

Feminism is a total war ideology. It is insufficient to simply fight a legal battle, or push for moderate changes in the media or pop culture. On the contrary, feminism requires holistic top-to-bottom assaults on every single aspect of our 'male-dominated patriarchal, oppressive' society. It's quite impressive actually. Maybe they are more like men than we thought. They attack masculinity by labeling it toxic, they eradicate male-only spaces by infiltrating the Boy Scouts, they demonize young men by creating rape culture. And whether by ill intent or happenstance, male biology is even under siege, where the very essences of maleness, testosterone levels, and sperm counts, are at generational lows.[6768] The war is comprehensive and continues unabated.

IV

FEMINISTS ELECT TO be blind when it comes to differences between men and women despite data, science, and plain old common sense. When you observe a man and woman together, the differences between them are apparent. Men are generally taller, stronger, and can impregnate a woman. Women are smaller, weaker, and can grow babies inside them. It seems reasonable to assume natural differences in desires and attitudes would arise from such physical differences. Our bodies and minds are inextricably linked, and we've evolved to maximize our unique capabilities. A division of labor allows for specialization and growth. Surely, a different mindset is required to nurse a newborn baby, compared to say, protecting the nursing mother.

Our hormones drive these physical differences and they also influence our thoughts and feelings. Any woman who has experienced a menstrual cycle can attest, the effect hormones have on their brains can be overwhelming. Same goes for young men living through peak testosterone production. It's almost as if the body takes over decision making for the time, driving them to seek out sexual partners and release. These hormones don't just change our bodies, they drive observable differences in male and female behavior across countries and cultures, spanning different eras and epochs, and finding roots in our archetypal stories and shared mythologies. Simply put, understanding men and women are different is foundational to humanity. Without our dimorphism, without our physiological differences, without the clear distinctions between men and women, there would be no people. To some readers this will sound perfectly obvious, yet to others, it will seem like unfettered misogyny.

When transgenders transition from female to male, the first thing they do is take male hormones. These hormones drive physical changes like a deeper voice and more facial hair. The transgender desires congruence between their gender identity and their physical body. So they change their body through hormones, but these hormones also affect the brain. Higher levels of testosterone change the way humans think, act, and feel. There is little dispute that more testosterone leads to higher levels of aggression, risk-taking, and sexual appetite. Any man who has supplemented his own testosterone production with exogenous injections will tell you the same thing. Higher testosterone changes behavior into actions we primarily associate with being male. Men with low testosterone who elect for testosterone replacement therapy are seeking its transformative effect on mood and behavior as well as on the body. Injecting yourself with testosterone is like injecting yourself with masculinity. Trans people experience the same changes upon beginning therapy. Hormone supplementation is a foundation of sexual transition. It's almost as if science has determined "maleness" can be created through drugs that mimic substances found naturally... in men.

If feminists and transgender advocates support sexual transition through hormones, you would think they could see the biological determinism of gender. Men produce far more testosterone than women naturally, trans women seek out testosterone to become men, and this testosterone leads to changed behaviors. The vast majority of the world's testosterone comes from the male testicles. The phrase "have enough balls" to do something probably comes from an acknowledgment long ago, that male behavior is driven by male biology.

But feminists today reject biological essentialism. They don't believe men act like men because men are built like men. They believe men act like "men" because society tells them how to think, feel, and act. They believe gender expression is a social construct rather than a result of biology. They use this same argument to claim cultural expectations of females shape their gender identities as well. There is no consideration that a woman's body, her hormones, or her role in reproduction could influence her gender identity. There is no mind-body connection for feminists. The more radical of them even claim men and women are biologically the same. It's as if our hormones and biology have no meaning unless a woman wants to become a man. In that case, hormones are essential to sex and gender.

The preposterousness of the transgender issue made me ashamed to have called myself a Democrat. The plain hypocrisy of their arguments, their commitment to ignoring science and reason, and the willingness to impose these disturbing views on children revealed the moral bankruptcy of the left to me and millions of other people. Seemingly overnight, an entire network enabling sex transition appeared in the United States, complete with a public relations strategy and a National Geographic cover story normalizing transgenderism and gender reassignment. Children are now offered hormone blockers pre-puberty to prevent sexual maturation. Parents are taught to coach children into gender dysphoria rather than therapy. As a result, transgenderism is now considered socially contagious as peer pressure and societal conditions urge children to adopt a transgender mind frame. What once evolved over an extended period now arrives as "rapid onset."[69] And the newly created transgender industry is waiting, ready to castrate and mutilate sick, confused people. It is disgusting and shameful. Democrats and their feminist supporters sacrifice the health and well-being of children at the altar of politics.

Feminists push the transgender issue because it helps them chip away at biological essentialism. Anything that looks like a nonconforming expression of gender allows feminists to argue that women are equal to men in every capacity. In their quest for equality between men and women, feminists are willing to destroy both sexes along the way. Issues which accelerate the obliteration of traditional gender roles are natural allies to feminists and the Democrats. They co-opted the transgender issue and exploded it into a national matter, despite only a negligible portion of the population experiencing gender dysphoria. Beyond logic, science, and reality, what feminists and trans advocates failed to take into account was that the trans issue eviscerates their own positions.

In the rush to promote anything that seems to aid in the erasure of typical gender expression, they ignored the most critical element of the matter: it is impossible to be born the wrong social construct. This bears repeating: If gender is a social construct, you cannot be born the wrong gender. Feminist theorists must choose: either gender is a social construct, and therefore transgenders are a logical impossibility, or transgenders are real, and therefore gender is something you're born with. Feminists don't care for logic or science. Apparently, they only care about their agenda: destroy men and everything related to them, including ideas of masculinity.

I have deep empathy for people who suffer gender dysphoria. They deserve our love, care, and kindness. They especially deserve mental health services which aid them to a peaceful resolution of the disturbance in their mind. What they don't deserve is a fast-track to body mutilation. Most cases of gender dysphoria in young people fade away with time as people work through their issues and into a stable understanding of who they are. And in any case, an adult human can choose to do whatever they like to their bodies, dress however they want, and behave in whatever way makes them comfortable. My outrage is reserved for when transgender politics gets applied to children.

I had a friend who expressed gender dysphoria as a child. She dressed like a boy, acted like a boy, even took on a typical male name. She played tackle football in the mud while other girls wore dresses and went to ballet.

We had a name for that back then, she was a 'tomboy.' But, over time, she realized she didn't want to be a man. She didn't want to live with a man's name, dress like a man, or even act like one. When she matured, she realized she was indeed a woman and was happy to live that way. Had she expressed gender confusion in 2017, she may very well have been herded into a reassignment center, given hormone blockers to prevent full sexual maturation and possibly been mutilated through surgery. What a tragedy that would have been. Confused tomboys and fairies today aren't so lucky. Instead of given time to develop their own identity, they are rushed into rash decisions and physical harm. Transgenders and feminists prioritize their agenda over the well-being of kids. Children are now collateral damage in the culture wars, which reveals a particular madness surrounding us.

When rational people witness irrationality, they find it disturbing. A glimpse into a chaotic world isolated from reason and science brings a visceral aversion. Watching other humans flail around in the darkness of unhinged thinking makes those of us who value order and reality feel unsettled. Today, we are watching a delusion acted out upon society and our fellow humans. When we encounter a single instance of insanity, it is easy to write off and look the other way, but when the lunacy descends upon half the country, infiltrates our institutions, and takes over our universities, we sane people are deeply troubled. We are so deeply troubled that we are willing to take risks to end the insanity. And in 2016, the risk we took was electing Donald Trump as president over Hillary Clinton, the Queen Feminist herself.

For nine million Democrat to Deplorable voters, Donald Trump was a beacon of hope amidst a frightening sea of chaos. Had Hillary Clinton become President, the feminist armies would have marched unmolested across our country, accelerating the loss of science, reason, and reality. More sacrifices would have been made to the equality gods. More children would have been mutilated. Our world would have dipped one layer deeper into the black abyss of unreason and horror. A Clinton victory would have lifted feminist theory to the highest office and used that power to spread its lies and terror into every aspect of American life. Democrats who voted for Obama, people like me, people who respect gay rights, civil rights, and equality of opportunity for all people, saw what Clinton would enable and we had to do something. Nine million of us broke ways with our old party, the party we proudly supported, to save the country from sanctioned insanity. Donald Trump and his uber-masculine persona, model wife, and swashbuckling business approach, represented the necessary counterweight to lead the country back from the edge of chaos and into the realm of order. In 2016, a vote for Donald Trump was a plea for a return to reality, a re-embrace of reason, and a prayer that it wasn't too late.

V

SINCE THE '90s, feminism has comingled with other ideologies on the way to its current perversion. Feminism metastasized into intersectionality, which in turn gave birth to social justice and its warriors. These social justice warriors spread into society with their marching orders: patriarchy is bad, masculinity is toxic, objective reality is a myth, lived experience is the only truth, science is white supremacy, biology isn't real, men and women are the same, and anyone you disagree with should be shouted down, shamed, shunned and silenced. There is no questioning the foundational myths of the social justice warrior. If you merely wish to discuss the assumptions or the data, you're a wretched misogynist and anti-diversity. If you doubt their conclusions, you're part of the patriarchy. And if you refuse to kowtow to their demands, they unleash the mob on you.

Our current condition is a result of a fusion between social justice warriors, feminism, and post-modernism. Post-modern philosophy believes there is no objective reality and our individual realities are mediated by language. This means they believe each person has a unique reality, one that can be controlled and manipulated by the words they use. They think language creates reality, rather than reveals a reality which exists independently of human observation. Social justice warriors wish to alter reality and therefore want to use the power of law to govern what we say. In California, it is now illegal to use the 'wrong' pronoun in certain situations.[70] In Canada, politicians have criminalized wrong speak as well.[71] It is now literally illegal to speak the wrong words. That these laws arise around transgender or non-binary gender identities is no accident. The post-modern left wishes to obliterate the idea that men and women are different, and they attack all elements of communicating about gender as a way to achieve their goal.

Feminists and post-modernists have also now fused with the Marxists. Marxists see the world in terms of power struggles between capitalists and workers. When real-world experiments failed, and Marxism had no economic arguments left to make, Marxist theory then slithered into feminist theory, where it has been appropriated with enthusiasm. The feminist version of Marxism believes the patriarchy defines our culture, that men oppress women, and the only way to remedy this is to annihilate the patriarchy and the men who comprise it. Male power is now considered the bourgeoisie, while females are the proletariats. Consistent with Marx's revolutionary ideas, the true liberation of women can only come at the defeat of the male-dominated patriarchy, or so the theory goes.

We should wonder what might happen if the feminist, Marxist, post-modernist axis of evil were to achieve victory. Marx called for revolution, stealing the bourgeoisie's property, and stripping them of their rights. He believed the source of their power was property rights, rights which had to be abolished to bring freedom to the working class. In today's world, men are the bourgeoisie and their political and economic power comes from their inherent masculine power. Therefore, the only way to 'free' women from the patriarchy is to destroy masculinity. Once maleness is brought to its knees and denuded of its power, the proletariat feminist will consolidate their new authority and use it to create a utopia. When feminists and social justice warriors talk of smashing the patriarchy, this is what they mean: the end of male power and the rise of female authority. Have you ever seen the t-shirt favored by feminists that says, "The Future is Female"?

Hillary Clinton was the leader of this revolutionary alliance of feminism, intersectionality, post-modernism, and Marxism. The "I'm with HER" slogan made her campaign all about her vagina and gender expression as a woman. She rallied this new cult by using the language of feminism and intersectionality on the campaign trail and by validating their grand myths of the wage gap and rape culture. Did Hillary understand how this mishmash of ideologies aims to destroy the foundations of Western

Civilization? Did she realize promoting feminist ideology meant advancing the decline of the West? We can only speculate about her knowledge of the issues, but smashing the patriarchy, controlling language, abandoning science, and forgetting about rationality will indeed lead to an erosion of western values.

Perhaps the scariest element of the Marxist/feminist/post-modern alliance is the erasure of the individual. To intersectionalists and their allies, the individual is subsumed by the group identity. Your unique characteristics, interests, desires, intellectual capability, physical capability, or biology are all less important than your group membership. Race, gender, ethnicity, age group, sexual identity - these are the defining human traits today. Enlightenment ideals of reason, rationality, and the primacy of the individual are now less important than the color of your skin. In a world defined by power dynamics between the oppressor and the oppressed, who you are as a unique individual is far less important than where you lie on the power spectrum. Marxists believe culture and all its ideas are a result of economic conditions, intersectionalists believe group identity is paramount, and both views discard the individual as irrelevant.

This tension between the cult left and Western Civilization is unresolvable. The cult left believes Western Civilization is a male-dominated patriarchy which oppresses women and minorities. And that patriarchy is created by, defended by, and supported by straight white guys. The only way to free the oppressed people is to destroy the source of Western Civilization and its defenders: white dudes. This conflict is built into the core of the intersectional ideology. Without oppressors, there is no oppression. For intersectionality to exist, it must not only identify additional sufferers but also maintain and preserve the notion of oppression. Intersectionality fused with Marxism and post-modernism is by definition a lethal threat to Western Civilization.

All of which makes it odd Hillary Clinton decided to be Queen Feminist and court the cult left in her campaign. The United States is the pinnacle of Western Civilization. At this point in history, our culture has won the Darwinian wars of natural selection and risen to the top. An informed, rational thinker cannot comprehend those who support ideologies antagonistic to the ideals of the West. Why bother running for President of the United States if part of your voting base wishes to destroy it? Hillary didn't just dog whistle to the cult left, she adopted their language, their posture, and promised her victory would be theirs. It's almost as if a vote for Hillary was a vote to end culture as we know it.

Our collective understanding of feminism is backward-looking, focused on the righteous achievements in civil rights, believing feminism is about suffrage and independence, rather than the annihilation of civilization.

But for those of us who see the trajectory of these ideologies, blissful ignorance is not an option. War footing is the only reasonable posture. To attack is the only winning strategy. Passive observation is surrender, and surrender leads to the end of the West. This war will define our future, write the unwritten history of America, and in turn, decide the fate of our great civilization.

THE BLUE CHURCH

THROUGHOUT THIS BOOK I've described to you faceless specters who are responsible for your growing ill-ease. I've written about amorphous groups with toxic ideologies. And I've presented arguments for ethereal enemies which strive to break down your sense of reality. This collection of forces work every day to control your mind, your ideas, and your feelings. Their power comes from stories or narratives that confuse and scare you. If you feel like there is a network of people, ideas, and organizations striving to manipulate and control you, you're not crazy. In fact, your daily life is subjected to a sophisticated network of influencers who work in tandem to push their agenda right through your eyes and ears and into your heart and soul. That network is called the Blue Church, and the Blue Church has made it clear, you're either with them, or against them.

I first heard of the Blue Church idea from writer, thinker, CEO, and technology expert, Jordan Greenhall. His essay, *Understanding the Blue Church*, published in March, 2017, is the best summary of this phenomenon I've read.[72] He explains,

> "[T]he Blue Church is a kind of narrative / ideology control structure that is a natural result of mass media. It is an evolved (rather than designed) function that has come over the past half-century to be deeply connected with the Democratic political "Establishment" and

lightly connected with the "Deep State" to form an effective political and dominant cultural force in the United States.

"We can trace its roots at least as far back as the beginning of the 20th Century where it emerged in response to the new capabilities of mass media for social control. By mid-century it began to play an increasingly meaningful role in forming and shaping American culture-producing institutions; became pervasive through the last half of the 20th and seems to have peaked in its influence somewhere in the first decade of the 21st Century. It is now beginning to unravel."

At first, the Blue Church evolved to solve a problem. Life is more complex today than ever before. It is faster-paced and better connected. Technology has created new opportunities for learning, trading, and sharing. Plus, the population in the United States has exploded, increasing from 30 million in 1860 to 300 million in 1960. So, not only is everything more complicated, but we have more people than ever magnifying the complexity.

Greenhall claims one of the most important technological evolutions of the 20th century was the emergence of the mass media like radio, newspapers and broadcast television. And while the various forms of media are different, they all have one thing in common: they are asymmetrical. A tiny group of people create the content that a massive group of people consume. Mass media is a top down distribution of ideas that flow from an exclusive group in control, to the faceless millions called the audience. Messages come down from the top and the masses listen.

This process, according to Greenhall, makes society a coherent group aligned around particular narratives. In other words, it turns millions of individuals into one entity.

This isn't always a bad thing. There is simply too much data out there for us to absorb and process. When a trusted source, like the friendly evening news anchor, tells us how to behave and why, it's only natural for us to listen. It is efficient and rational to act this way. Sometimes it's good to be handed a road map and told to follow. Doing so creates national cohesion needed to manage the tricky process of getting us all on the same page.

> *"This is the formal core of the Blue Church. It solves the problem of the 20th Century social complexity through the use of mass media to generate manageable social coherence."*

When broadcast media took off in the '60s, the format created a model which persisted over time and spread into other forms of media. Walter Cronkite is a great example of the top-down, informed to uninformed, teacher to student model of information distribution. Cronkite would sit at his desk and tell us the news, and therefore what was important. He'd tell us how to think and feel through unidirectional broadcasting of his one message to millions of people. The Cronkite method primed us to be receptive to messages sent down from the mountain top.

The Blue Church organized us around particular narratives and also conditioned us to seek out and trust asymmetric information systems such as university educations, government messages, and political propaganda that reflected Cronkite's effect. Sanctioned information authorities tell the uninformed what to think. In a world where information exploded along with the population, we needed guidance. There is comfort in familiar models. Teachers, authority figures, governmental leaders, and corporate giants seem trustworthy to the children of the Blue Church because they follow the same pattern: top down dissemination of what to think and feel.

People born in the '60s and '70s grew up with this system and in time they became leaders in our society. The children of the Blue Church brought an unrelenting faith in the top-down information model to their positions in academia, industry, and government. They were raised on stories from movies and TV shows laced with political ideas and propaganda that spread common narrative across the country. And because the Blue Church has always been dominated by the Democrats, the children of the Blue Church are predominantly progressive types. They brought a leftist world view and supreme faith in the narratives to their new found positions of power.

Today, the Blue Church is everywhere. It's the collection of government agencies, media companies, ad firms, tech giants, wall street financiers, universities, Human Resource departments, and just about every other organization which shapes our culture today. Their leaders, their adherents, and their customers all drink the same blue Kool-Aid. We know what their narratives are, we've discussed them throughout this book. They are ideas like the wage gap, rape culture, the benefits of globalism, the value of group identity over individual expression, and of course the foundational myth: that every human being on the planet is exactly the same. And don't forget, the Blue Church evolved as a way to manage social coherence, so if you question these narratives you are met with shame, ridicule, and exile.

The coercion tactics of the Blue Church play on our needs as social animals. We all desire membership in a social group. One way we identify which group we are in is by which stories we believe and adhere to. When broadcast media transmits the latest updates to the story lines, we have a tendency to accept them, mostly because we believe everyone else in our group is doing the same. If you reject the narrative, then you are recanting your group membership and are no longer one of "us" but one of "them."

I was shunned by my tribe during election 2016 because I asked questions about the dominant narratives. My friends and family responded to my curiosity with shame and ridicule. Once I signaled that I didn't believe any longer, I was quickly pushed aside, abandoned by the people I thought were my closest friends. But generally, our urge to belong to an identifiable social group is powerful, so powerful that we forget to be critical of the myths which brought us together. Humans can engage in sincere self-delusions and an uncritical acceptance of the group mythology is one way we fool ourselves.

The Blue Church has dominated control over the access to information until recently. The old media's job was to find new information and distribute it to the uneducated. But this process isn't a free and liberal system where all ideas get equal attention, there is too much data for that. So the Blue Church curates, or choses, what information gets sent around and in the process becomes a filter for truth. The stories they tell us become our realities, and because we're only hearing a portion of the data, we're also only seeing a portion of the truth. Thus, if we are forced to rely upon the top-down distribution model of the Blue Church, our understanding of reality is flawed. The mass media's monopoly on information gathering and distribution has been so strong they could pass partial truths and half-realities off as the big picture, dominating the national narratives and in turn, the country.

But the Blue Church monopoly on information distribution and control is breaking. Digital technologies like blogs, Twitter, YouTube, and Periscope have disrupted the existing media universe. In the past, the capital and expertise required for broadcast technology prevented anyone but the media companies from sharing information. But today, a mobile phone has replaced the television studio and information has been liberated from the Blue Church's gatekeepers. The internet provides access to the entire universe of available data, and at the same time provides a cheap and easy way to distribute that data to large numbers of people. The Blue Church's stranglehold on truth and reality is breaking, and new ideas are emerging. But when they do, the Blue Church rallies to squash them using their trusted techniques of shame, ridicule, and exile. As new media liberates more information, there will be more skirmishes between the old line Blue Church and the emerging red resistance.

I

HUMAN RESOURCE DEPARTMENTS are on the front lines in the Blue Church's war on competing ideas. In the past, the Blue Church used social stigma as way to control thinking and behavior. People were afraid to stray from the party line for fear of becoming an outcast. If all your friends thought one way, but you decided to think differently, that usually meant you were going to be alone. But this abstract notion of losing your group membership is nowhere near as powerful as the tools the Blue Church has today.

Now, HR departments are staffed by the children of the Blue Church and armed with the same tools of shame and exile. But instead of just losing a group of friends, you can now lose your job. Rather than a television screen broadcasting the Faith while you passively receive it, the HR department in 2018 enforces cohesion through diversity and inclusion workshops, implicit bias trainings, equity assurance programs and unspoken quotas. And if you break ranks, or even just ask a few questions, HR has the ultimate weapon: termination. It's a newer, more personal method of indoctrination and it is a particular danger for Democrat to Deplorable voters.

Take for example James Damore, the young man fired from Google for expressing a dissenting view.[73] The Diversity, Integrity, and Governance team at Google was working to root out sexism in their workplace. The believed sex-based discrimination lead Google's workforce to skew more heavily towards men rather than an exact proportion of 50% male and 50% female. To remedy this situation, Google created a series of workshops and events to eliminate oppression and find ways to work towards sex-based parity. Their assumption being, all men and women are the same, enjoy the same things, have the same preferences, and therefore should desire to work in all fields equally, which would result in a 50/50 split of employees at Google.

After one such workshop, the Google team requested feedback from the participants. James, an engineer and biologist by training, took that request to be a genuine desire to discuss the science and ideologies behind Google's diversity initiative. So he went home and researched differences between men and women, pulling together a number of resources which show, through peer-reviewed studies, that men and women are in fact different with different dispositions, different interests, and even different personality traits.

As requested, he wrote up his findings in a formal paper and presented the feedback to the Google community. In his report he suggested hiring and employment outcomes may not necessarily be the direct result of the patriarchy oppressing women, or a white supremacy culture keeping minorities down. Instead, Damore wondered if average group differences between men and women might be the reason fewer women work in tech than men. He considered the idea that women make their own elections based on personal preferences. And that these choices explain the different numbers of men and women at Google, rather than blaming a nefarious conspiracy keeping women out.

In sum, he credited women with the capability to make their own choices. This line of thinking, ascribing agency and individuality to women, an individuality which may lead to different outcomes than men's, violates the foundational myth of the Blue Church: all people everywhere are exactly the same, including their preferences and life choices. To question this in the Blue Church is to out yourself as a heretic. Deviance from the myth, especially backed with science from credible sources, is prohibited. Even though Google asked for his feedback, they didn't really want it. His paper challenged the world view of those in charge and therefore it deserved only shame, ridicule, and a purge.

Outrage ensued.

Despite never once being cited by HR for discriminatory practices, or being known as a sexist, Google fired

James for sharing his paper. Not only was James fired but he was publicly shamed for reporting on existing research, research which to any reasonable observer, is non-controversial. James made the ultimate mistake. He failed to understand the request for feedback was an empty one, that critical consideration of all sides of an argument was undesirable, even anathema to the cause. He questioned the fundamental tenet of the Blue Church: all people are the same, everywhere, at all times and for that he endured the Blue Church's ultimate consequence: exile.

93% of Democrat to Deplorable voters believe: "It seems the Democratic Party does not encourage free thinkers or new ideas."

The story of Damore's firing exploded onto the national scene and the Blue Church pulled out its usual guns to fight back. The media apparatus decried his memo as a misogynistic screed, a manifesto of hate, and the embodiment of everything wrong with men today. Blue Church news sources circulated his memo only after deleting the citations, making it appear as though he conjured up the idea that men and women may be different. They purposefully omitted the science behind his assertions because the Blue Church does not play fair. They play by only one rule: dissent must be incinerated. Truth, facts, science, and the fate of a normal, harmless, programmer at Google are irrelevant. The narrative must be maintained at all costs, even at the expense of integrity. Truth is the enemy of the Blue Church. It eviscerates their core principles and therefore it must remain hidden.

What happened to James Damore was a perfect example of why Democrat to Deplorable is happening. The entire fiasco embodied the culture war perfectly. The memo addressed many of the issues we face around gender. It challenged the first principle of the cult left, that everyone everywhere is the same. Then Google's behavior revealed itself as a political entity with a dangerous perspective. Damore's termination demonstrated what happens when you deviate from the corporate political agenda: you get fired. There is a word for when you are fired for political beliefs, it's called persecution. All other groups and their views are protected. If you support a liberal agenda and push those beliefs on everyone around you, all good. But if you dissent, you're in serious jeopardy.

Because we've rejected the Blue Church and embraced an alternative perspective, Democrat to Deplorables are now an unprotected class in America whose jobs, livelihoods, and even personal safety are at risk. We are unprotected by the same laws which provide comfort to those who tout the party lines. If you deviate from the dogma of the Blue Church you are a heretic, or worse, an apostate. And there is nothing more dangerous to a cult than one who renounces the faith and embraces the other side, which is exactly what Democrat to Deplorable voters have bravely done.

II

As the Blue Church begins to lose grip on the national narratives, new political parties are forming. The old lines of liberal and conservative are losing their meaning. Democrat to Deplorable voters are the vanguard of this change. Today the world is dividing between truth seekers and science deniers. The schism begins with our mutually exclusive understanding of the nature of men and women.

The Blue Church believes men and women are exactly the same, they have the same capabilities, they have the same preferences, and in all circumstances can produce the same outcomes. Some even believe men and women are biologically the same. This belief tumbles downward from religious proclamation into government policies, corporate hiring practices, and academia. It then commingles with other perverted ideas like post-modernism and mutates into sinister formulations like intersectionality, which lead to dangerous tribalism and conflict. It is difficult to overstate the ramifications of male-female equalism for it is the basis of the Cult of Equality and therefore the beginning of our culture war. The Blue Church rejects any notion of gender essentialism, or the idea our biology influences behavior.

The truth seekers, on the other hand, begin with the understanding men and women are different, that our observable biological differences in form and function also influence our behaviors, attitudes, and preferences. We don't believe one version of human is better than the other, they are just different. And those differences are required elements of humanity. Our very existence depends on the reproductive differences between men and women, why would our mental and emotional make-up be different? We are a collective animal, working together in groups to achieve common goals. If everyone was the same in every way, our evolution would be impeded. Ironically, to believe in the differences between men and women is to believe in the power of diversity, while a belief in their sameness rejects it.

The Blue Church rejects what we see with our eyes, and instead preaches belief in a mystical universe where nothing is better than anything else.

As the leftists move to enforce an equality of outcomes for all, rather than the equality of opportunities, the world shatters into two irreconcilable factions. On the left, they believe everyone is the same and therefore all <u>outcomes</u> should be the same, whereas the right appreciates human differences and believes all <u>opportunities</u> should be the same. For the left, it's not enough to simply give everyone the same chance with equal protections under the law, equal opportunities for education, careers, and family life. Instead, they prefer to coerce everyone into the same outcomes, an inherently illiberal notion which rejects the primacy of the individual and considers people only as members of collective groups, never mind the impossibility of forcing people to perform in a predetermined way. Your group membership defines who you are and what you should be. There is no room for individual expression and the variance of outcomes that occurs when folks are left to express personal preferences and indulge in their unique desires. When you combine this collectivism with gender equalism, the result is the expectation that everything for men and women should be the same, and if it doesn't turn out that way, it can only be because of one terrible horrible thing: the patriarchy.

Let me be clear: forcing people with inherent differences into equal outcomes is a form of slavery. It is torture. It is the dehumanization of one person to achieve an arbitrary and ill-founded utopia where all people are exactly alike. How will you induce people to go against their nature? How will you force people into the outcomes the government decides? This isn't just about men either, women are victims in this scenario, too. How do you make women work in computer science when they'd rather teach elementary school? How do you force them to take sanitation or construction jobs, when they'd rather be nurses? Unless the left abandons the notion that everyone is the same, the internal logic of their arguments inexorably leads to totalitarian compulsion. It may take brainwashing, torture, or draconian penalties to coerce people into professions they have no interest in. Top down decision making in the lives of individuals is antithetical to our Democracy, liberty, and Western ideals.

Ultimately what's dividing us here is Nature vs. Nurture. The deciding factor for Democrat to Deplorable voters was a re-embrace of nature, a return to biology and an escape from socially constructed ideas about socially constructed reality. We are voters who changed, we endured a transformation, one we began as the left dragged us all closer to a total abandonment of nature and objective reality. A move away from nature is a move towards chaos, and chaos is a terrifying, bewildering place, a place where men are women and women are men and the first fundamental truth we understand is obliterated, leaving us unanchored and tossed about.

Have you ever stared into the black sky, looking between the stars and wondered what was out there? Has the vastness of time and space ever felt overwhelming when you attempted to consider the scale of infinity? We've all become burdened at one time or another with the understanding that we are nothing when compared to the universe. A hopelessness can fill the void in our minds created by the thought of never ending time or ever expanding space. Without a barrier between ourselves and the chaos of infinity, we become chaos ourselves.

For protection from the unknown we begin by defining the known. And man's relationship with woman is a first step in creating a safe space to navigate. Big vs small.

Father vs mother. Penis vs vagina. Mastery of these differences gives us a secure mind space in which to rest. The physical connection made during sex is a manifestation of the mutual understanding of men and women, where we acknowledge our differences, define who we are by sensing what we are not, and then unite into one versus the world. Obliterate the differences between men and women and lose the first true safe space humans ever created. Without the security of our first understanding, the remaining belief structures collapse, leaving us naked and alone against the universe. Is this a bit melodramatic? Perhaps. But philosophies which ignore our basic human nature ignore nature itself and that is a dangerous way to live. The evils of the world don't rest simply because you refuse to acknowledge them.

Our job as humans is to try and make sense of the unpredictable while protecting ourselves from the negative forces of nature. Roofs over our heads are the same as scientific understanding in that both offer relief from the chaos of nature. Any ideology that chips away at the roof will be met with revulsion and disdain, as it should. Forces that tear down barriers between chaos and order are our natural enemies, just as anyone who builds a wall to protect us from the creatures of the night are our heroes. Herein lies the battle for reality which dominated the presidential election. There is a culture war afoot and this war is over a choice. The choice is do we erect and maintain barriers between us and chaos? Do we continue to build order in the face of the wild? Do we keep ourselves out of the rain? Or do we tear down the walls which keep us safe and invite the chaos in?

In Moby Dick, Herman Melville 's character, Pip, discovered what it's like to be without any barriers between us and nature. When he fell out of the crow's nest and into the ocean, left behind by the ship in the middle of the night, doomed to bob in an infinite sea of darkness, he understood the natural state of humans in nature. With nothing below, around, or above but the infinity of the sea at night and the blackness of space, Pip's head exploded as he encountered the true condition of man. Man is helpless against nature, man is meaningless against nature, man is subsumed by nature in every way. Bobbing along in a cold dark sea under a starless black sky, with no ships on the horizon, no islands to swim to, no floor to stand on, the isolated man in the heart of nature returned to the only place a human mind exposed like that can go, to the horrors of insanity. When one directly engages the infinite the only reasonable outcome is madness. A man in the chaos of nature cannot be a man, he can only be chaos. For what partially defines us as humans is our ability to withdraw from the chaos, erect barriers between us and it, and to begin the process of understanding nature in order to render it less powerful before us.

ARE VOTERS THINKING about *Moby Dick* when they make their decisions? Of course not. Most people spend little time pondering the nature of the universe and where the various candidates fit into larger philosophical terms. Everyday Americans are focused on important surface concerns like jobs, health care, and immigration. But this doesn't mean the grander ideas have no influence. We just are generally unable to articulate our thoughts and feelings on existential questions, despite them motivating us to act in certain ways. We humans are capable of analyzing large quantities of data and do most of the information crunching below the surface, where the results manifest themselves as hunches, or feelings emanating from our gut. If you've ever made a decision and explained yourself by saying, "I don't know, it just felt right," you know exactly what I mean. Our body draws a conclusion and then spurs us to act through feelings.

The information war today is being fought in our subconscious. The Blue Church has mastered the art of transmitting neat little packages of data where the surface level message is easily understood by the brain but the deeper more powerful message gets transmitted directly to the body. Similar to interpersonal communication, the overt message may say one thing, but the hidden sub communication tells another. Good persuasion doesn't just rely upon the top level message, it works by sending the listener bigger more powerful messages wrapped in easily swallowed bits of believable truths.

A great example of this phenomenon is the wage gap theory. The Blue Church continuously pushes the notion that women get paid less for the same work as men. It's symbolized by the easily remembered meme of women are only worth 77% of men. Embedded in this digestible nugget of information is a universe of influential data.

Contained within the wage gap meme are several assumptions. It assumes someone is tracking wage information and this information is accurate. It assumes there are bad people who see a woman's name on the job application and automatically decide they can pay her less. The hiring managers are then supported by their corporate masters, or more likely, are forced by them to discriminate against women. It's not just an isolated misogynist oppressing women, it is an active conspiracy working to keep women down. The bad people get together and think, how can we oppress women, how can we make them worse off than men today? How do we keep women subservient to men?

The conspiracy is driven by hate and an urge to guide material benefit and advantages to men, even at the expense of corporate profits. Hiring men and paying them more for the same work women can do is economically irrational. Therefore, the bad people out there are willing to sacrifice profits and financial success for the chance to oppress women. Because the wage gap is pervasive, this means our entire economic system is an irrational conspiracy designed to hurt women. And finally, the wage gap meme presumes men and women are precisely the same, with the same motivations and the same capabilities. If men and women should be paid the same, then presumably they are equally capable and willing to do the same exact work in the same exact amount of time and as a result, get paid the same exact wage. And the only thing standing in their way is the patriarchy.

That is a lot of information underneath a simple statement, but there's even more. Embedded in the critique of the wage gap is the notion that we must do something to fix it. Fixing it includes getting rid of all the bad people, changing the way they think, and revolutionizing the way companies hire and pay people. It means mental reconditioning, it means widespread change, and it likely means some level of retribution. Bad people get punished in the United States, and what could be worse than oppression?

Of course none of this is spoken when the 77 cents meme is distributed. All we hear is that women get paid less than men. Once the surface level idea enters your brain, the remaining embedded assumptions, proclamations, and ideologies unfurl into your subconscious. The meme asks no permissions before installing itself into your operating software. Our brains are like open-source computers, susceptible to outside programming, and these dense memetic packages, like the wage gap, are laden with viruses which creep into the deep recesses of your mind without your knowledge or acceptance. Because the deeper messages bypass the conscious brain, they are processed by the subconscious and then reveal their presence in the form of emotions or visceral feelings. These feelings motivate people to act, either in support of the meme, or against it. And in the case of the wage gap, because the underlying ideology is a false one, where men and women are precisely the same, the result is a dissonance which feels like discomfort, fear, or even rage.

Here the Blue Church made a big mistake. They believed they could pummel men with lies long enough that they would succumb and submit. They underestimated the power of the dissonance caused by stories which demean reality and erode our understanding of men and women. They miscalculated when they thought they would have perpetual control over the narratives and information flow. The Blue Church's success over the last several decades blinded them to the receding power of their dominant position. Instead of a docile and amenable population ready to give in to the lies of the Blue Dogma, the Blue Church now faced a rage-filled insurgency empowered by the liberation of information.

The scorched earth tactics of the left ensured the only thing remaining in opposition were the very things they hated: strong, powerful, masculine men, men who reject the Blue Church and are immune to its tools, the sort of men with the stamina and constitution for revolution. This revolution was latent, waiting until the right moment to rise up and resist. All these insurgents needed was a weapon to combat the monopolistic power of the Blue Church, and by 2015, they were armed, ready, and mad as hell.

IV

I'VE MENTIONED MARXISM a lot throughout this book because Marx's ideas still have buoyancy with the cult left, feminists, and so-called progressives who make up the Blue Church. They see Marx's main idea of wealth (power) redistribution as a good and worthy goal. But history has proven that Marxism is fatally flawed and deadly to its adherents. The utopia promised by Karl Marx never came to fruition. Collectivism ended in mass murder, the breakdown of the state, and cultural turmoil. Its elevation of the group over the individual is anathema to our Western ideals. By all accounts, a Marxist society of state controlled economics, cultural fascism, and no property rights would be contrary to all the things Americans hold dear: freedom, liberty, and the right to pursue whatever we want. Yet, despite its failing as a practical way to organize society, the Marxist framework still has some value as a tool for analysis. What follows is a review of the new media revolution seen through the lens of a Marxist model.

For Marx, the economic mode of the time defined all relationships in society including familial, political, and economic. The people who controlled the means of production therefore controlled the remainder of society as well. If you owned the factories and controlled the capital necessary to finance them, you controlled the country. The rest of us, the proletariats, were left to succumb to capitalist domination for survival. To Marx, this was a condition of slavery, a world where workers had no rights and were subjects of the factory owners, or bourgeoisie.

The mode of economic production was seen as a power struggle. Those with the factories had all the power and the workers had none. This lead to exploitation by one class over another. The only way to free the workers of the world was to "liberate" the means of production from the bourgeoisie. In other words, revolution was the only answer. And that answer involved eliminating the source of the bourgeoisie's power: property rights. Without property rights, the factory owners could no longer enslave workers and from there a utopian paradise would spring forth, showering freedom, prosperity, and liberty on all, or so the theory goes.

In today's world, information is the true currency of power. We live in a semi-capitalist, semi-Democratic country where control of companies and country can change hands. Competition provides incentives for challengers to rise, and dominant forces to resist. Part of the American dream is this idea of class and power mobility. New companies form, rise up, and take control. Old companies which fail to evolve fade into the past. Political factions grow in prominence, and recede from power. There is an ebb and flow to who owns the businesses and controls the government. But one thing has remained the same for many decades: the Blue Church controls information production and the means by which to distribute it.

Seen through a Marxist framework, today's relationships and society are determined by who controls the means of information production. The media conglomerates, working together with academia, government, and the deep state, control what narratives we are told, what news stories we see, and ultimately what we should believe. He who controls information controls reality. And because there is too much information for individual humans to process, we rely on other people to tell us what is important. We allow them to guide our attention to their priorities, accepting their version of reality, irrespective of its true value or personal relevance. In this way, the dominant Blue Church is the new bourgeoisie. They control the means of information production and its distribution. Therefore they control the relationships which make up our society.

There is no escaping the torrent of information. In the past, everyday Americans got their news through a local newspaper or small town gossip. Radio, television, and then mass media of all kinds increased the number of news sources exponentially, and they permeated all aspects of our daily life. News and information was once something you sought out, but today, it finds you. If you are somewhere where goods and services are sold, you cannot escape the push of information. Try walking down the street without absorbing unwanted data. Try driving across the country without seeing or hearing advertising. It's impossible. Televisions, tablets, smartphones, public video screens, marketing. We are saturated with information in ways unfathomable to folks just a few decades ago. Today truly is the Age of Information. In Marxist terms, the "economic mode of production" has been surpassed by the "information mode of production" as the salient factor in today's culture.

The ways information is created and distributed are Marx's "means of production." Those who control what content we see, and how we engage with it, have all the power. Your information diet forms the foundation for your mental framework, just as the food you eat provides the building blocks for your physical health. In many ways, he who controls the narrative, controls your mind. The Blue Church understands this and uses it to reinforce their ideologies, their control, and their power. Information is the dominant force and those who control it are the dominant class.

The power dynamic described by Marxist theory is exploitive, and the informational balance of power today is no different. Mass media and the Blue Church prey upon people's inherent rational ignorance. The effort required to verify information we encounter takes too much work, so we rationally accept much of which we see, read, and hear as accurate. The big companies with their political agendas know this to be true and overwhelm us with waves of information, drowning our ability to discern the truth. When the Blue Church uses its media channels to deliver dogma, they know we can't defend ourselves. The proletariat in the information age is defenseless against this tsunami approach. Until the internet and emergence of social media, the power accrued to the Blue Church bourgeoisie was incontestable. The proletariat was a slave to the system, and the Blue Church bourgeoisie was the master. Only a revolution could free them from the oppressive power structure of the Information Age.

The internet and social media arrived and provided the tools for the informationally oppressed to rise up and begin the resistance. Previously, journalists, media companies, research institutions, and academia all acted like gatekeepers to the truth, keeping some information sequestered behind an opaque wall of curation. Editors, funders, and content creators with an agenda carefully selected what information the masses were allowed to learn, understand, or even discuss. Information consumers felt like they had a choice, proactively choosing what to consume, but really they were limited by the given options. It's like when a parent says to a child, you can have broccoli or green beans, which would you like? The child thinks they're making a choice, but really they're just enjoying the illusion of freedom. It was the same when the Blue Church offered you information. You made your selection from a stacked deck.

But the internet changed all of that by removing the gatekeepers, eliminating the curators, and shortening the distance between raw data and consumer. Today, anyone with a laptop and an internet connection can deliver information to the masses, unimpeded by previous obstacles like printing presses, distribution channels, and the massive investment required to acquire both. The tools of the information age provided the weapons of revolution. Technological advancements shattered the monopoly of the new bourgeoisie, offering the once ignorant information slave the chance to break free, a chance to discover alternative voices, content, and yes, even alternative facts.

What happens when individuals find themselves holding the tools to a revolution? What happens when the mass media loses control over how information is created and distributed? Tiny pieces of resistance begin to form and sprouts of revolution begin to appear. Nodes of insurgent life begin to rise up and bring new information and new thinking. Individual people, small businesses, and anyone with motivation can now report news and info to the entire world. This information, now unfiltered by the gatekeepers of the past, is free in ways never seen before. The old line media companies have lost the power of curation; their choices of what we can see and hear are no longer the only narratives we rely on to consider reality. The independent content creator can produce freely, the distribution channels are (relatively) agnostic, and the active consumer elects how, where, and when to receive the information they desire. The means of information production and consumption have been transformed, and with it, the power dynamics of the old way are eroded. An information revolution has arrived and the Blue Church bourgeoisie is giving way to the proletariat of the red insurgency.

V

So, NOW WE'VE seen what the Blue Church is, how they came to power, and what they've done to preserve their dominant position. We've also looked at the ways in which the Blue Church's power is being diminished through the evolution of new forms of media and communication. And now, we're going to talk about you. You, are what evolves in a world dominated by the Blue Church. You, are the only thing that can withstand the onslaught of the Blue Church's shame and ridicule. You, are America's last chance against the vile and corrupt ideologies of the Blue Church. You, are the soldiers of the culture war. You, are the Red Resistance.

The Red Resistance is the result of decades of Blue Church control. The hegemonic dominance of the Democratic establishment and the institutions they operate has created a unique reaction. The emergence of the Red Resistance is owed to the defining characteristics of the Blue Church. The only type of resistance that could withstand a generation of the blue plague, is the only resistance which can conquer it. You were born of the Blue Church and eventually you will kill it.

The grand narratives of the Blue Church forced us to create counter narratives that defined our new group. Men and women are the same (no they're not). Nurture is more powerful than Nature (no it isn't). Equality of outcome is more important than equality of opportunity (false). And don't forget rape culture (fake), the wage gap (a lie), and globalism over nationalism (wrong).

When we spoke out against the Blue Church mythology, we were silenced and pushed further to edge. The Blue Church does not allow dissent. Questions or curiosity about alternative viewpoints are met with humiliation and ejection. When the Blue Church of Google discovered James Damore was freethinking, he was fired and exiled because debate is unnecessary and undesirable. As the Blue Church clamped down harder on dissenters, they accidentally emboldened us. Damore stayed true to his views, was labelled a hateful sexist misogynist, and yet survived to fight another day. He was bold enough to question the Blue Faith and lived to tell about it. Damore, and others like him, are survivors of the Blue Plague because he was immune to their tactics. People like Damore are all that's left. The Blue Church has smothered all other opposition and the only group which has survived is the Red Resistance. Like you.

Jordan Greenhall explains:

"Yet, even as the Blue Church was achieving dominance, the roots of the Insurgency were being laid. And, like bacteria becoming increasingly immune to an antibiotic after constant exposure, those aspects of the emergent "Red Religion" that were able to survive at all began to coalesce and expand. What has now erupted into the zeitgeist is something new and almost

completely immune to the rhetorical and political techniques of the Blue Church. To call an adherent of the Red Religion "racist" is unlikely to elicit much more than a "kek" and a derisive dismissal. The old weapons have no more sting."

"[T]he Insurgency evolved within a culture broadly dominated by the values and techniques of the Blue Church and therefore, by simple natural selection, is now almost entirely immune to the total set of 'Blue critique...'" [74]

We are all survivors. Lisa faced the Blue Church's shame in her personal life and survived. When her friends called her a Nazi, she brushed them off. Sarah had actual battles with the Blue Church, and now she is even happier. Dimitri withstood the incredulousness of his family and friends to vote red in 2016. And I myself woke up one day and realized all the people in my old life hated me... but somehow I didn't care. We each became immune to the Blue Plague, which labels all resistance as racist, bigoted, Nazi scumbags. The Blue Church's tactics no longer had power over us and once we realized that, we proceeded ahead with pride rather than shame.

The weapons of the Red Resistance were born out of competition with the Blue Church. They are independent blogs, Twitter, YouTube, Facebook, and even email lists. The democratized information landscape delivers us new information, alternate points of view, and data that was once hidden. The Red Resistance uses the digital media universe to find information directly from sources and distribute it directly to audiences. These new technologies allow us to observe, react, and respond to the Blue Church faster and more cohesively than before. Think of the way news breaks across Twitter and into your timeline. As soon as one member of the Red Resistance knows something, we all do.

This unification around information creates a powerful community. And it is an essential tool in resisting the Blue Church. They use the fear of isolation and exile to herd you into compliance. But now the Red Resistance short-circuits these tactics by fluidly moving out of the hostile blue group and into an accepting red tribe. Remember earlier in the book, when I described the online communities I discovered after my divorce? It was then I first realized the immense power of finding new communities online. I was able to make new connections with people I'd never met before. We came together to share ideas and experiences. When we connected we felt less alone, less isolated, less confused and less afraid. Divorce can often lead to exile from the marital community, so finding a place to belong becomes important. Online communities can ease the transition to a new life.

The same thing happens for members of the Red Resistance. Before the internet, shame and exile from the Blue Church meant social death. This made people very afraid to cut against the gospel. But now that there are alternative communities we can join, ones that are united by ideas instead of by geography, we've found a new strength. We are no longer silenced by fear of isolation. We Deplorables sought out new associations and relationships based around ideas, ideas that ran counter to the dominant narratives. These were the ideas that earned our exile from the Democrats. Revolutionary ideas.

The Deploraball was a highlight for our growing community. There at the National Press Club our crew got together to share smiles, ideas, and support. This new community enabled more Deplorables to come out of the darkness and into the light of friendship. We were able to replace the sense of social cohesion we lost when we were evicted from the Blue Church with a newer, better, more accepting social group who understood and appreciated us. For many of us, the Deploraball was the moment we emerged from the wilderness to discover our new home.

The Red Resistance is a direct response to the decades long dominance of the Blue Church. The media, tech giants, institutions, universities, and the deep state are all die hard members of the Blue Faith. They are the ruling forces in America, and the Red Resistance are the revolutionaries. The Blue Church is the evil Empire, and we are the scrappy rebels in a desperate fight. The Blue Church is vile, dishonest, and oppressive, while the Red Resistance fights for freedom, liberty, and the American way of life. America is depending on you and the Red Resistance to withstand the Blue Church and to Make America Great Again.

Acknowledgments

I interviewed countless people for this book and I'd like to thank them for taking the time out of their busy lives to speak with me. Special thanks to: Greg, George, Dimitri, Lisa, and Sarah for the hours of interviews and phone calls and amazing stories.

Thanks to my good friends Dennis, Mike, and Will for their insight, guidance, and friendship.

Thank you to my three beautiful children for being patient while I "wrote words in the basement."

To my mom for her eternal support and unconditional love, thank you.

And to Rachelle, this book would not be what it is without you. Thank you for your tireless coaching, expert editing, and overwhelming support. I loved working with you and I'm proud of what we've done.

Appendix

Basic Demographics of Survey Respondents:

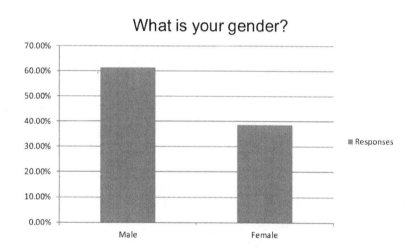

What is your gender?

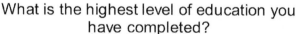

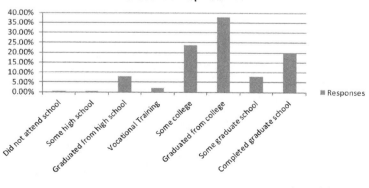

What is the highest level of education you have completed?

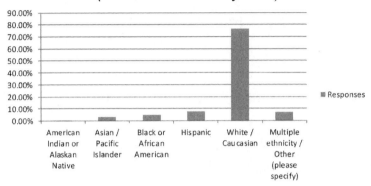

Which race/ethnicity best describes you?
(Please choose only one.)

How old are you?

What is your approximate average household income in a typical year?

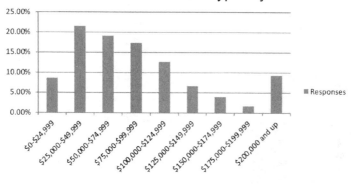

Which of the following best describes your current relationship status? (Choose all that apply)

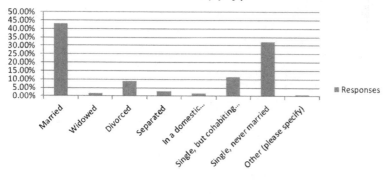

Do you have any children under 18?

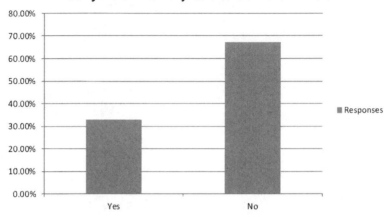

What is your sexual orientation?

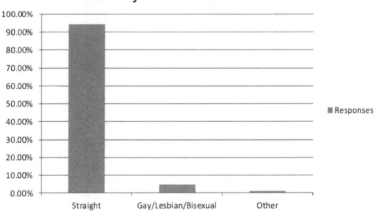

Do you identify with any of the following religions? (Please select all that apply.)

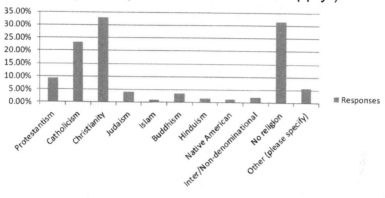

Endnotes

1 "Wish You Were Here." Recorded 1975. In *Pink Floyd*. AAO Music, 1975, CD.

2 *Equal Opportunity in the Fort Wayne Community Public Schools* - A report prepared by the Indian Advisory Committee to the U.S. Commission on Civil Rights, July 1979.

3 "Who Initiates Divorce More Often?" Psychology Today, accessed May 02, 2018, https://www.psychologytoday.com/us/blog/the-third-wave/201705/who-initiates-divorce-more-often.

4 Rollo Tomassi, *The Rational Male* (Nevada: Counterflow Media LLC, 2015).

5 Livingston, G., & Cohn, D. (2012, November 29). U.S. Birth Rate Falls to a Record Low; Decline Is Greatest Among Immigrants.

6 Cohn, D. (2011, December 14). Marriage Rate Declines and Marriage Age Rises.

7 *Wendy Wang and Kim Parker, 2014. "Record Share of Americans Have Never Married: As Values, Economics and Gender Patterns Change." Washington, D.C.: Pew Research Center's Social & Demographic Trends project, September.*

8   US Census Bureau. "Commuting Times, Median Rents and Language Other than English Use." The United States Census Bureau. December 07, 2017. Accessed April 29, 2018. https://www.census.gov/newsroom/press-releases/2017/acs-5yr.html.

9   All schools in Washington receive equal funding per student from the local government. But the richest neighborhoods use their PTA's to raise funds and supplement their public school's budgets, adding staff, equipment, and resources exceeding those of the unsupported schools on the other side of town.

10 "NEA - NEA Home," Rss, accessed February 29, 2018, http://www.nea.org/assets/docs/PB11_ParentInvolvement08.pdf.

11 White Supremacy Culture. Accessed January 25, 2018. http://www.cwsworkshop.org/PARC_site_B/dr-culture.html.

12 "What Is Suspicious Activity?" Department of Homeland Security, February 01, 2018, accessed April 30, 2018, https://www.dhs.gov/see-something-say-something/what-suspicious-activity

13 Selk, Avi (September 15, 2015). "Irving 9th-grader arrested after taking homemade clock to school: 'So you tried to make a bomb?'" *The Dallas Morning News*.

14 Kalthoff, Ken; Bryan, Ellen (September 15, 2015). "Irving Teen Says He's Falsely Accused of Making a 'Hoax Bomb'" nbcdfw.com

15 Katherine-mangu-ward. "Judge Upholds Suspension of the Pop-Tart Gun Kid." Reason.com. June 17, 2016. Accessed November 30, 2017. http://reason.com/blog/2016/06/16/judge-upholds-suspension-of-the-pop-tart.

16 Peter Hermann, "Protester Pleads Guilty to Conspiring to Disrupt DeploraBall for Trump Supporters," The Washington Post, March 07, 2017, , accessed May 30, 2017, https://www.washingtonpost.com/local/public-safety/protester-pleads-guilty-to-conspiring-to-disrupt-deploraball-for-trump-supporters/2017/03/07/3f55f-3da-0347-11e7-b1e9-a05d3c21f7cf_story.html?utm_term=.830e632faf37.

17 At the time of publication. Alex Fields, Jr, the man accused of killing Heather Heyer with his car in Charlottesville, Virginia in August, 2017 was still awaiting trial.

18 Josh Meyer et al., "FBI, Homeland Security Warn of More 'antifa' Attacks," POLITICO, September 01, 2017, accessed September 03, 2017, http://www.politico.com/story/2017/09/01/antifa-charlottesville-violence-fbi-242235.

19 Rosie Gray, "The 'New Right' and the 'Alt-Right' Party on a Fractious Night," The Atlantic, January 20, 2017, accessed January 30, 2017, https://www.theatlantic.com/politics/archive/2017/01/the-new-right-and-the-alt-right-party-on-a-fractious-night/514001/.

20 Andrew Marantz, "The Alt-Right Branding War Has Torn the Movement in Two," The New Yorker, July 06, 2017, accessed July 10, 2017, https://www.newyorker.com/news/news-desk/the-alt-right-branding-war-has-torn-the-movement-in-two.

21 Rasmussen_Poll. "Just How Many Obama 2012-Trump 2016 Voters Were There?" Rasmussen Reports. Accessed July 30, 2017. http://www.rasmussenreports.com/public_content/political_commentary/commentary_by_geoffrey_skelley/just_how_many_obama_2012_trump_2016_voters_were_there.

22 "The U.S. Dropped an Average of 3 Bombs per Hour Last Year," NBCNews.com, accessed May 01, 2017, https://www.nbcnews.com/news/world/u-s-bombed-iraq-syria-pakistan-afghanistan-libya-yemen-somalia-n704636.

23 Jessica Purkiss and Jack Serle, "Obama's Covert Drone War in Numbers: Ten times More Strikes than Bush," The Bureau of Investigative Journalism, March 28, 2017, accessed May 01, 2017, https://www.thebureauinvestigates.com/stories/2017-01-17/obamas-covert-drone-war-in-numbers-ten-times-more-strikes-than-bush.

24 David Krayden, "Hillary Clinton Now Blaming Obama Legacy For Election Loss," The Daily Caller, November 22, 2017, accessed December 01, 2017, http://dailycaller.com/2017/11/22/hillary-clinton-now-blaming-obama-legacy-for-election-loss/.

25 "Table 1. Work Stoppages Involving 1,000 or More Workers, 1947-2017," U.S. Bureau of Labor Statistics, February 09, 2018, accessed April 01, 2018, https://www.bls.gov/news.release/wkstp.t01.htm.

26 "Table 1. Work Stoppages Involving 1,000 or More Workers, 1947-2017," U.S. Bureau of Labor Statistics, February 09, 2018, accessed March 01, 2018, https://www.bls.gov/news.release/wkstp.t01.htm.

27 Perry Bacon Jr., "How Arne Duncan Reshaped American Education and Made Enemies Along the Way," NBCNews.com, January 02, 2016, accessed March 01, 2018, http://www.nbcnews.com/meet-the-press/how-arne-duncan-reshaped-american-education-made-enemies-along-way-n480506.

28 Megan Messerly, "Sanders Wins Most Delegates at Clark County Convention," LasVegasSun.com, April 02, 2016, accessed March 01, 2018, https://lasvegassun.com/news/2016/apr/02/sanders-wins-most-delegates-at-clark-county-conven/.

29 Report. http://www.p2016.org/chrnothp/Democracy_Lost_Update1_EJUSA.pdf.

30 Tessa Stuart, "WTF Happened at the Nevada Democratic State Convention?" Rolling Stone, May 17, 2016, accessed May 01, 2017, https://www.rollingstone.com/politics/news/wtf-happened-at-the-nevada-democratic-state-convention-20160517.

31 Pennsylvania Elections - Summary Results, accessed May 01, 2017, http://www.electionreturns.pa.gov/General/SummaryResults?ElectionID=54&ElectionType=G&IsActive=0#.

32 Michelle Ye Hee Lee, "Analysis | Donald Trump's False Comments Connecting Mexican Immigrants and Crime," The Washington Post, July 08, 2015, accessed June 01, 2017, https://www.washingtonpost.com/news/fact-checker/wp/2015/07/08/donald-trumps-false-comments-connecting-mexican-immigrants-and-crime/?utm_term=.86a4ca084ac9.

33 "Entertainment," MarketWatch, accessed May 01, 2018, https://heatst.com/culture-wars/bias-incident-team-students-three-blind-mice-halloween-costume-makes-fun-of-a-disability/.

34 Anemona Hartocollis, "Yale Lecturer Resigns After Email on Halloween Costumes," The New York Times, December 07, 2015, accessed November 08, 2017, https://www.nytimes.com/2015/12/08/us/yale-lecturer-resigns-after-email-on-halloween-costumes.html.

35 The Center for Immigration Studies defines a sanctuary as, "cities, counties, and states [which] have laws, ordinances, regulations, resolutions, policies, or other practices that obstruct immigration enforcement and shield criminals from ICE - either by refusing to or prohibiting agencies from complying with ICE detainers, imposing unreasonable conditions on detainer acceptance, denying ICE access to interview incarcerated aliens, or otherwise impeding communication or information exchanges between their personnel and federal immigration offices."

36 Jackie Salo and Chris Perez, "Special-needs Man Tortured While Attackers Livestream It on Facebook," New York Post, January 06, 2017, accessed February 03, 2017, https://nypost.com/2017/01/04/special-needs-man-tortured-while-attackers-stream-it-on-facebook/.

37 Drew DeSilver, "For Most Workers, Real Wages Have Barely Budged for Decades," Pew Research Center, October 09, 2014, accessed September 01, 2016, http://www.pewresearch.org/fact-tank/2014/10/09/for-most-workers-real-wages-have-barely-budged-for-decades/.

38 Nicholas Fitz, "Economic Inequality: It's Far Worse Than You Think," Scientific American, March 31, 2015, accessed May 10, 2016, https://www.scientificamerican.com/article/economic-inequality-it-s-far-worse-than-you-think/.

39 Philip Bump, "Obama Calls Inequality the 'Defining Challenge of Our Time'," The Atlantic, December 04, 2013, accessed October 01, 2017, https://www.theatlantic.com/politics/archive/2013/12/watch-live-obama-takes-income-inequality/355783/.

40 Sheelah Kolhatkar, "The Cost of the Opioid Crisis," The New Yorker, September 08, 2017, accessed March 01, 2018, https://www.newyorker.com/magazine/2017/09/18/the-cost-of-the-opioid-crisis.

41 Olga Khazan, "Why Are So Many Middle-Aged White Americans Dying?" The Atlantic, January 29, 2016, accessed March 04, 2018, https://www.theatlantic.com/health/archive/2016/01/middle-aged-white-americans-left-behind-and-dying-early/433863/.

42 Adam Davidson, "Why Are Corporations Hoarding Trillions?" The New York Times, January 20, 2016, accessed February 01, 2018, https://www.nytimes.com/2016/01/24/magazine/why-are-corporations-hoarding-trillions.html?mcubz=0.

43 Ta-Nehisi Coates, "The First White President," The Atlantic, September 14, 2017, accessed November 01, 2017, https://www.theatlantic.com/magazine/archive/2017/10/the-first-white-president-ta-nehisi-coates/537909/.

44 Jon Henley, "Extend Border Controls to Counter Terror Threat, Say France and Germany," The Guardian, September 15, 2017, accessed April 01, 2018, https://www.theguardian.com/world/2017/sep/15/france-and-germany-seek-to-extend-limit-on-schengen-zone-suspension.

45 "Getting People Where the Jobs Are," Democracy Journal, September 19, 2016, accessed May 01, 2017, https://democracyjournal.org/magazine/42/getting-people-where-the-jobs-are/.

46 Noah Smith, "The Dark Side of Globalization: Why Seattle's 1999 Protesters Were Right," The Atlantic, January 06, 2014, accessed May 15, 2017, https://www.theatlantic.com/business/archive/2014/01/the-dark-side-of-globalization-why-seattles-1999-protesters-were-right/282831/.

47 Coletta Youngers, "The U.S. and Latin America After 9-11 and Iraq - FPIF," Foreign Policy In Focus, May 13, 2013, accessed October 01, 2016, http://fpif.org/the_us_and_latin_america_after_9-11_and_iraq/.

48 http://www.american.edu/ocl/orientation/upload/CDI-Challenge-Yourself.pdf

49 Harvard University News Office/Delacorte Press, "Psychology's Favorite Tool for Measuring Racism Isn't Up to the Job," The Cut, January 11, 2017, accessed May 01, 2018, https://www.thecut.com/2017/01/psychologys-racism-measuring-tool-isnt-up-to-the-job.html.

50 http://www.american.edu/ocl/orientation/upload/Title-IX-AU-for-students.pdf

51 Brian D. Earp, "1 in 4 Women: How the Latest Sexual Assault Statistics Were Turned into Click Bait by the 'New York Times'," The Huffington Post, September 28, 2016, accessed October 01, 2016, https://www.huffingtonpost.com/brian-earp/1-in-4-women-how-the-late_b_8191448.html.

52 Alexandra King, "Campus Rape Stats 'misleading,' Says Book Author," CNN, January 28, 2017, accessed February 01, 2018, https://www.cnn.com/2017/01/28/health/campus-rape-book-author-cnntv/index.html.

53 Campus Safety and Security, , accessed May 01, 2017, https://ope.ed.gov/campussafety/#/institution/details.

54 Emily Yoffe, "The Uncomfortable Truth About Campus Rape Policy," The Atlantic, September 06, 2017, accessed November 01, 2017, https://www.theatlantic.com/education/archive/2017/09/the-uncomfortable-truth-about-campus-rape-policy/538974/.

55 Greg Lukianoff and Jonathan Haidt, "The Coddling of the American Mind," The Atlantic, July 31, 2017, accessed August 01, 2017, https://www.theatlantic.com/magazine/archive/2015/09/the-coddling-of-the-american-mind/399356/.

56 "Where Microaggressions Really Come From: A Sociological Account," The Righteous Mind, April 20, 2016, accessed November 01, 2016, http://righteousmind.com/where-microaggressions-really-come-from/.

57 Steven Pinker, *The Blank Slate: The Modern Denial of Human Nature* (New York: Penguin Books, 2016).

58 "World News, Politics, Economics, Business & Finance," The Economist, accessed May 01, 2018, http://www.economist.com/news/international/21645759-boys-are-being-outclassed-girls-both-school-and-university-and-gap:.

59 Erika Christakis, "Do Teachers Really Discriminate Against Boys?" Time, February 06, 2013, accessed October 01, 2017, http://ideas.time.com/2013/02/06/do-teachers-really-discriminate-against-boys/.

60 "The NCES Fast Facts Tool Provides Quick Answers to Many Education Questions (National Center for Education Statistics)," National Center for Education Statistics (NCES) Home Page, a Part of the U.S. Department of Education, accessed May 01, 2018, https://nces.ed.gov/fastfacts/display.asp?id=72

61 Belinda Luscombe, "Workplace Salaries: At Last, Women on Top," Time, September 01, 2010, accessed May 01, 2018, http://content.time.com/time/business/article/0,8599,2015274,00.html.

62 Rob Wile, "Women Now Hold a Majority of All Management and Professional Positions in the U.S.," Splinter, April 07, 2015, accessed May 01, 2018, https://splinternews.com/women-now-hold-a-majority-of-all-management-and-profess-1793846899.

63 "BMO Report: Despite Controlling $14 Trillion in Wealth, American Women Still Have Challenges to Overcome," Marketwire, accessed May 01, 2018, http://www.marketwired.com/press-release/bmo-report-despite-controlling-14-trillion-wealth-american-women-still-have-challenges-tsx-bmo-2006436.htm.

64 "Census of Fatal Occupational Injuries (CFOI) - Current and Revised Data," U.S. Bureau of Labor Statistics, February 20, 2018, accessed April 01, 2018, https://www.bls.gov/iif/oshcfoi1.htm#2011.

65 Jill B. Becker and Ming Hu, Frontiers in Neuroendocrinology, January 2008, accessed May 01, 2018 https://www.ncbi.nlm.nih.gov/pmc/articles/PMC2235192/.

66 "QuickStats: Life Expectancy at Birth, by Sex and Race/Ethnicity - United States, 2011," Centers for Disease Control and Prevention, September 05, 2014, accessed May 01, 2018, https://www.cdc.gov/mmwr/preview/mmwrhtml/mm6335a8.htm.

67 *Human Reproduction Update*, Volume 23, Issue 6, 1 November 2017, Pages 646–659, https://doi.org/10.1093/humupd/dmx022

68 Journal of Clinical Endocrinology and Metabolism, January 2007.

69 "Misunderstanding a New Kind of Gender Dysphoria," Quillette, October 11, 2017, accessed May 01, 2018, http://quillette.com/2017/10/06/misunderstanding-new-kind-gender-dysphoria/.

70 California Senate Bill SB 219, Wiener. Long-term care facilities: rights of residents.

71 Canadian Bill C-16: An Act to amend the Canadian Human Rights Act and the Criminal Code.

72 Jordan Greenhall, "Understanding the Blue Church – Deep Code – Medium," Medium, March 30, 2017, accessed May 01, 2018, https://medium.com/deep-code/understanding-the-blue-church-e4781b2bd9b5.

73 https://assets.documentcloud.org/documents/3914586/Googles-Ideological-Echo-Chamber.pdf

74 Greenhall, Jordan. "Situational Assessment 2017: Trump Edition," January 25, 2017.

Made in the USA
San Bernardino,
CA